EliminateChaos

EliminateChaos

The **10**-Step Process
to Organize Your
HOME & **LIFE**

Laura Leist

SASQUATCH BOOKS
SEATTLE

Printed in Singapore by Star Standard Industries Pte Ltd.
Published by Sasquatch Books | Distributed by Publishers Group West
13 12 11 10 09 08 07   8 7 6 5 4

Cover photographs: Adam L. Weintraub (Kitchen), Marco Prozzo (Laura Leist)
Cover design: Nina Barnett

Kitchen featured in cover photograph:
Architect: Tom Nychay, Sortun-Vos, Seattle
Contractor: Cranston Construction, Seattle
Cabinetmaker: Spencer Horn, Seattle

Interior design and composition: Kate Basart/Union Pageworks
Interior illustration: Kate Quinby/Croak and Hum

Eliminate Chaos® is a federally registered trademark of Eliminate Chaos® LLC.
"It's Not About the Stuff" is a trademark of Eliminate Chaos.

Library of Congress Cataloging-in-Publication Data is available.

ISBN 1-57061-467-9

Sasquatch Books | 119 South Main Street, Suite 400 | Seattle, WA 98104 | 206/467-4300
www.sasquatchbooks.com | custserv@sasquatchbooks.com

CONTENTS

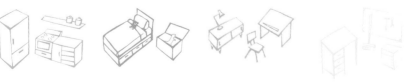

PREFACE

Laura's Story: "It's Not About the Stuff"

You can't take it with you when you go" is something my mom used to say to my brother, Scott, and me all the time when we were growing up. I now realize that the message she was trying to instill in us was this: Life is not about the material things we accumulate in our years on this earth. But as a young child, those nine words "You can't take it with you when you go" puzzled me. I didn't really understand them until one day about 20 years ago, in 1984.

My parents divorced when I was five and Scott was three, and they shared custody of us kids. Shortly after the divorce, Mom, Scott, and I moved to Washington; Dad and Ceil moved there a few years later, so we would all be close.

We settled into a modest three-bedroom, one-bath home with about 1,000 square feet of living space. The house had a detached shed but no garage. Needless to say, we didn't have a lot of room for extra, unnecessary "stuff."

In the early years of her marriage, Mom had been diagnosed with diabetes, a disease that meant she couldn't have children. My parents were intent on having a family, though, so they adopted Scott and me. Mom's diabetes didn't keep her from her other passion, either: she was a concert pianist, played the tympani in the symphony and jazz piano in a small band, taught vocal music at my elementary school, and gave private piano lessons in our home.

Most of Mom's work-related time was spent teaching piano lessons. While she taught, her purse always sat next to her on the floor. When she was finished with lessons for the day, she would take the purse with her to the kitchen while she prepared dinner. When it was time for bed, the purse would go with her to her bedroom. In the morning, when Mom was putting on her makeup, the purse would sit next to her chair by the dresser. It didn't really matter where Mom was in the house; her purse was always by her side.

By the time I was fourteen, Mom's health had started to deteriorate due to the many complications of diabetes. It was time for Scott and me to move to Dad and Ceil's house so Mom could concentrate on her health. Mom spent the next two years in and out of hospitals. I was too young to understand all that was going on.

In August 1984, Mom entered the hospital for the last time. She was there for about a month before being sent home in mid-September. When she came home, my grandma Marie, my mom's mom, was there to take care of her. On a Friday evening, I remember talking to Mom about the homecoming dance I was going to that night, and telling her that I looked forward to seeing her again on Sunday, which was the day before my grandma's birthday.

Unfortunately, during the wee hours of that Sunday morning, my dad received a phone call from Grandma Marie, the kind of call I'm sure no one could ever be prepared for. My mom had passed away, Marie told him, just a few hours before Scott and I were to see her again.

My dad had to deliver the news to Scott and me that morning, since we had planned to pick Mom and Grandma up for church. I cannot imagine the pain that Dad must have experienced, thinking about how he was going to deliver this news to his two children.

Later that morning, Dad took us to Mom's house, where both Grandma and Grandpa were waiting. During the 20-minute drive there, I had no idea what to expect or what I'd feel when I walked back into Mom's house. I was completely numb, my heart ached, and there was a knot in my stomach.

What I do remember is this: Grandma said to Scott and me, "Go ahead and take anything you want—it's all yours." I didn't really comprehend what I was hearing and instead wandered around the house aimlessly, as if Mom were going to reappear.

A short time later I wandered into Mom's bedroom, and there on the floor next to her bed sat her purse. Suddenly it hit me like a ton of bricks—"You can't take it with you when you go." Mom was right.

To this day, I have never forgotten those nine words and what they mean to me. Don't get me wrong; I like to have my "things" just as much as the next person. But I've chosen not to live a life of excess possessions after having witnessed firsthand the fleeting significance of "stuff."

It was impossible for me to take anything from our house that day. I was too overwhelmed by trying to understand how my mom's life had ended at the age of 46. But as the weeks passed, I found myself spending many hours at the house with Grandma and Grandpa, sorting through all of Mom's possessions and preparing for an estate sale.

Going through this process at such a young age no doubt helped me in more ways than I can recognize. For one thing, it taught me that in every tragedy, there is a learning opportunity. It may not always be obvious at the time, but eventually it becomes clear.

I truly believe the organizational gifts I have to offer today arose out of this formative experience. Many of our clients come to our company, Eliminate Chaos, because of frustration with one form or another of chaos in their life. They have no idea, when they share their very personal stories with me, how deeply I understand. I hope that after reading this book, they'll know that their project is more than just another job for me; it's about helping them create the kind of life they want to live.

During the countless hours we spent sorting through everything in my mom's house to prepare for the estate sale, I had a lot of time to reflect on the experiences we had shared. In the end, I kept only those things that meant the most to me, and let everything else go. I can count on the fingers of two hands the number of items I took. My list may surprise you. Here it is:

1. **Most of the photos,** which Scott and I have since divided between us.

2. **Most of the Christmas ornaments,** which Scott and I also divided.

3. **Mom's sewing machine**—and yes, I still use it today, although not as much as I'd like, since I'm running a business!

4. **Some of Mom's piano music** (mostly the books I used to play from while growing up, and a few pieces that evoke memories of Mom playing).

5. Mom's recipe box, containing her handwritten recipes (which I later computerized).

6. A few of her Hummels, which Scott and I divided.

7. The china, which to this day I don't think I've ever used; it sits packed away in the rafters of my garage. I think it may be time to let it go.

8. Several pieces of jewelry, some of which I wear, others of which I've kept for the memories they evoke.

9. The treble clef lamp that sat on our grand piano, which now sits on my piano in my living room, next to a photo of my mom and me.

10. Mom's black sapphire cocktail ring, which is the one item that I have today that I did not take from Mom's home. Rather, I had completely forgotten about it. When I graduated from college some six years later, my dad gave me a small jewelry box. Inside the box was this ring. A part of Mom was now with me on my graduation day. It truly was an amazing and thoughtful gift.

It's interesting to look at the above list and see what, among all my mother's possessions, proved most important to me—and what brought back the most memories. As you've probably already observed, most of the items on the list aren't worth much monetarily. But they're priceless in terms of the joy they bring to me.

Christmas was always a favorite time of the year for me when I was growing up, and decorating the Christmas tree was my favorite holiday activity. Mom, Scott, and I would unpack all of the ornaments, many of them handmade, and lay them out on the couch. Scott and I would then get to take turns selecting our favorites to hang on the tree. Each year we would get new ornaments, one for each of us. It was always so much fun to unpack them each Christmas. Today, as I decorate the Christmas tree each year, I still lay out all of the ornaments on the couch and reminisce about my childhood Christmases. For me—as for many of us, I think—it truly is the small things that mean so much.

Throughout my home, I have small reminders of my mom, in the few special treasures from our home and her life that I've kept. With the exception of her china, which is packed away, everything is being used or displayed. I don't have excess things from Mom's house packed up in boxes in my garage or storage area, because those things were just not important enough for me to keep.

You may wonder if I ever regret not having more. The answer is no. There was only one other item in our house that I would have loved to have kept—our grand piano, on which Mom taught lessons, and which I played as a child. For storage reasons, keeping it was quite impossible. Do I miss it? Sure, but again, it was just an object. More important are the memories I still have today of my mom playing the piano.

I share this personal story with you because, as you read this book, I want you to know that I understand how terribly difficult it can be to part with items that mean so much to you. And I want you to know that you can learn how to live without so much stuff.

This book is a little different from other organizing books. I wanted it to be full of practical tips but also personal stories. In the pages that follow, I'll share with you how real people have used my unique 10-step organizing process to achieve their goals, from being able to find things in their closets to giving their preteen son a bedroom he really likes (and can keep organized).

You'll read their true stories, see our actual shopping lists and budgets, and marvel at the before-and-after transformations. Each chapter also discusses common problems and offers additional organizing tips to help you make the most of your space. And the "Shopping Resources" appendix at the back of the book will tell you where to find the products we used. With this combination of the personal and the practical, I hope to show you how profound an impact getting organized can have on your life, and to inspire you to get started!

As you use this book as your guide to eliminating chaos in your home and life, keep in mind what matters to you most. Most people tell me it's the memories that mean the most—I know that was true for me.

DEDICATION & ACKNOWLEDGMENTS

I dedicate this book to my parents. As an organizing consultant, I truly believe that part of the reason I have the skills to do this work every day is because of my upbringing. Although my parents were divorced and I spent my childhood in two different homes, both homes provided structure, a sense of where things belonged, and systems for getting things done. And they both nourished my compassion and desire to help others.

Many people think I inherited my organizational skills, because I have very organized and successful parents. The truth of the matter is that I am an adopted child who learned from my surroundings. If you're one of the many people who have given up on your clutter because organizational skills are "not in your genes," I'm here to tell you that these skills can be learned. And this book will begin to teach you.

I want to thank the hundreds of clients I've worked with over the past five years. Each one of you has provided me with an opportunity to better my skills and come up with even more creative ways to help eliminate chaos in people's lives.

Thank you also to my staff, past and present, especially those who helped pick up the extra pieces while I dedicated six months to writing this book.

On a final note, I owe a big thank you to Rob. Without his daily support, help, words of encouragement, and love, I would never have finished this book while running a business.

CHAPTER 1

THE ORGANIZING PROCESS

What does it mean to be organized? Let's start with a couple of definitions. *Webster's Dictionary* definition of organize is "to give definite structure, arrange, put in working order."

My definition is "to make things efficient and functional" and "to make sure everything has a home." Organizing is not about shuffling things around; it's about taking an honest look at what you have, keeping what you need, letting go of the rest, and organizing what's left.

Organizing is a process, not an event. The chaos and disorganization you may be experiencing in your home or life didn't get there yesterday, and unfortunately it can't be eliminated tomorrow. The good news is, it will take you less time to get your home and life organized than it took you to get to your existing situation.

The process I've developed after working with clients over the past five years consists of 10 simple steps. These steps can be used to organize one room or an entire house. On page 4 is a list of these 10 steps, which you can use as a quick reference guide while you're organizing your home.

Before discussing each of these steps, let's go over what not to do.

TWO MAJOR MISTAKES MADE WHEN ORGANIZING

Many times, people tell me that they tried to organize their home, or a particular room in their home, but they gave up because it just didn't turn out right. Typically, the project did not turn out as expected for one of two reasons. There are two major mistakes that many people fall victim to that you won't make now that I've listed them here.

1. Shopping first.

Just about everyone loves to shop. For many people, shopping is the most enjoyable part of any organizing project, because it doesn't seem like work. As you'll notice from our 10 steps, shopping is step 8 on the list. If you love shopping as much as I do, think of it as your reward for doing a great job on steps 1–7! When we get to step 8, we'll discuss why it's important to wait to do your shopping.

2. Losing focus.

This mistake can best be illustrated by the real-life example of my client Maggie (not her real name), whom we organized for a TV program several years ago. The program sent us in to do a kitchen organizing makeover, and we had just seven hours. We started Maggie's kitchen makeover with a quick walk-through of her entire home. We needed to see the rest of the house so that as we found things in the kitchen that didn't belong there, we could create stacks of items to be moved to other areas.

When we were ready to start the kitchen, we began by opening all of the cupboards and drawers to get a good look at what we were dealing with. As Joyce, one of our Eliminate Chaos consultants, and I began to empty the cupboards, we noticed that Maggie was starting to pick up things that didn't belong in the kitchen. Then she started to leave. When we asked her where she was going, she told us, "I'm going to go to the basement to put these things down in my husband's workshop."

"Not so fast," I responded. Maggie flashed me a look. Why was she not being allowed to leave her kitchen? After all, it was her home. I quickly explained that part of the reason we take a quick tour of the home is so that we know where things belong. We fill separate boxes with those things and then deliver them to each room when we're done with the kitchen. If she were to leave the kitchen and go to the workshop, I explained, there would be a very good chance she would find something down there that didn't belong. Then she would take that item to the room where it belonged. Once there, she might find something else that needed to be done, and we would never see her again!

Maggie looked at me as if a light bulb had just been turned on in her brain. "So this is why I never get anything done," she said. "I just go from one room to the next. I keep busy all day long, but I never complete anything."

Maggie couldn't have summarized it better. After living in her home for 30 years, wondering why stuff was still everywhere, I think she was beginning to see the light!

Can you relate to this story? If so, please keep it in mind as you go through the 10 steps. It's important to stay focused on the current task and complete it before moving on to the next. Trust me, you'll feel a huge sense of accomplishment.

Now that we have the two major mistakes out of the way and I know you aren't going to make them, we're ready to talk about the 10 steps to organizing any room in your home.

TEN STEPS TO ORGANIZING ANY ROOM IN YOUR HOME

If your plan is to organize your entire house rather than just one room, I suggest that you start with the room that's causing you the most stress and making you feel the most overwhelmed. Please recognize that you can't organize an entire house all at once. You need to do it one area at a time.

1. Dedicate time.

How many times have you said to yourself, "I'll get organized someday" or "I'll get organized when I have more free time.'" I don't know about you, but the calendars that I use don't have the words "someday" and "free time" on them. Being organized is a lifestyle and a choice, so if you want to be organized, you must make it a priority and dedicate time for it.

When I say dedicate time, what I mean is that you need to write this event on your calendar. Make an appointment with yourself to work on the particular area that you've chosen. Think of this time as an investment in yourself.

Recently a good friend of mine, Kim, who wants to start a business, told me that she never has time to work on her ideas to get the business off the ground. Since she is a full-time mom to three children, I have no doubt as to why she has no time. I told Kim that what she needs to do is schedule the time with herself for this task, just as she schedules the time to exercise. It's a simple concept, yet many people fail to schedule time for what they really want to accomplish.

Have you scheduled a time for organizing on your calendar yet? If not, put this book down (I know that's hard to do!), and go do it. Once you have, I want you to think of this time as an appointment with yourself that you can't break. Resist the urge to reschedule the appointment if something more fun comes up (it always will). As with a lunch with a long-lost friend or a doctor's appointment, you can't afford to miss this time with yourself to make an investment in your life.

Another thing to keep in mind, when scheduling time with yourself to organize, is that the organizing process typically takes longer than you estimate. If you think your project is going to take two hours, I'd plan for four. If you think your project will take eight hours, I recommend that you plan for sixteen and break it up into several bite-size pieces that can take place over a period of time. As we've already discussed, organizing is a process. During that process, there will be many decisions to make. Some will be simple and quick, while others will be more challenging and take more time. I want to make sure you have enough time to complete your project.

Here are a couple of good rules of thumb for determining the amount of time needed for any organizing project:

◆ Multiply by 2 the amount of time you think it will take you to complete a project. That should give you a more realistic estimate.

◆ If you have a difficult time making decisions, multiply by 3 the amount of time you think it will take you to complete a project, and that will be your realistic estimate.

2. Gather supplies.

Gathering supplies is often confused with step 8, which is shopping. As you already know, shopping is the treat you earn by doing the hard work up front.

In this step, the supplies I want you to gather are items you probably already have at home:

- A garbage can (a large one is best) and/or several garbage bags

- Several boxes, paper garbage bags, or plastic storage bins in various sizes, to sort things into, including donations, recycling, and items that need to be taken to other rooms. (If you don't have any empty boxes lying around your home already, you could call your local grocery store early in the morning and ask them to save boxes for you. Later in the day, they're already flattened.)

- A shredder, or a box to hold paper to be shredded later (if you'll be working with paper)

- A thick marking pen, for labeling boxes

- Pen or pencil for writing

- Sticky notes in different sizes, for labeling

- Paper, for making notes

- Tape

- Something to drink (you'll get thirsty!)

Finally, make sure you're wearing some comfortable clothes that you don't mind getting dirty.

With your supplies gathered, you're just about ready to begin organizing! There's just one more step to complete before you really start working with your belongings.

3. Establish a staging area.

It's important for you to locate an area in your home, close to the area you're organizing, where you can place items as you begin. You don't want to trip over things while you work. Take it from me—I once broke a foot while organizing a client's garage and ended up in a walking cast for eight weeks. Not much fun, especially considering that I'm on my feet all day organizing with clients!

Do yourself a favor and make sure that you have a place to spread things out. Not only will it keep you from stepping over things, but you'll also find it much easier to see what you have and what you're sorting. Here are some examples of staging areas:

Kitchen: Use a kitchen or dining room table, or use folding tables if you have them. You could also use the floor, but you may want to lay down a sheet first.

Closet: Use the bed, the floor, or possibly the hall outside the bedroom. If using the floor, you may want to lay down a sheet first.

Home office: Use other rooms close by, or even the hallway.

Garage: Use your driveway or yard.

Donations and garbage: Be sure to have your garbage bins and donation boxes close at hand, no matter what room you're organizing.

4. Sort.

At last, we come to sorting—the step that will make you feel like you've finally begun organizing your things. This is one of the most important steps in the process. You must know what you have in order to organize, and this won't be possible unless you sort through your belongings. Sorting and the next two steps, purging and grouping like items together, can all be done at the same time, but it's important that each of the three steps take place.

Beginning the sorting process can be one of the most overwhelming parts of organizing, because it's difficult to know where to start. I want the sorting process to be as painless for you as possible, so I offer you these thoughts: There's no right or wrong way to begin; you just need to pick a place and get started. Eventually you're going to touch everything in the area that you're organizing, so it doesn't matter where you begin. If the room you're organizing is bursting at the seams, then it's even more important to establish the staging area so that as you begin sorting, you can remove items from the room you're working in, thus giving you more space. Don't worry about the fact that you'll be making an even bigger mess as you begin to sort. I do this all the time when I'm working with clients. Everything will eventually be given an established place, or "home." Sometimes just starting at the door and picking up the item closest to you, then making a *decision* about that item, is the best way to begin.

Ah, the word "decision." Let's take a brief moment to discuss decision making. You'll soon find that organizing is all about decision making. You need to decide whether you're going to keep, donate, sell, or throw away each item you have. As Barbara Hemphill states in her book *Taming the Paper Tiger at Home*, "Clutter is postponed decisions." I couldn't agree more.

As you're sorting through your belongings, please keep this concept in mind. As you pick up each item, make a decision about whether you're going to keep, donate, sell, or throw away that item. If it's to be thrown away, put it in the garbage immediately, before you allow yourself to touch and pick up the next item. If the item is to be donated, place it in your donation box.

Sorting this way will allow you to complete what I call "follow-through" with each item—resist the urge to look at the next item until you've made a decision about the current one. In my five years of working with clients, I've learned that people are easily distracted. They'll look at me, start wondering what I'm going to touch next, and set down the item I had handed them to make a decision about. Remember, follow-through is the key here.

5. Purge.

Do you have the urge to purge? Purging is a part of the organizing process. You don't need to keep everything you own. If you hold on to everything, you'll soon discover that you're out of space, and things will begin to stack up around you. Eventually you may end up with only narrow paths through your home amid all of your belongings.

Here are several good rules of thumb to keep in mind while determining what to keep and what to let go:

◆ Honor and cherish those things you keep. If they're buried in the back of the closet or in a box in the garage, you may have them, but how much enjoyment can they bring you in such an out-of-the-way location? Think about this as you're sorting through things and deciding whether to hang on to them.

◆ If you haven't worn an article of clothing in a year, chances are you never will, so it's time to let someone else have it. An exception might be special-occasion clothing that's worn only once or twice a year—but if you've been hanging on to special-occasion clothing for many years and it is out of style, it's probably time to let that go as well. See chapter 3 for more tips on letting go.

◆ If you haven't used an item in a year, you probably don't have a big need for it. Sure, there are a few things you'll use only on a yearly basis, and those items are certainly acceptable to hang on to—provided, of course, that you have the space to do so.

TIP

You may want to set up more than one donation box. For example, if you want to make donations to several different places, it will be much more efficient to immediately put each item in the box for that location, rather than to put them all in one box and then divide them up later.

◆ If you can't see something, chances are you don't know you have it. Think about this if you have piles of items that you're uncovering for the first time in a long time. How long have you lived without them and gotten along just fine?

As we're all aware, we have only so much time to accomplish everything that we want to do while we're here on earth. Be realistic about the projects you're hanging on to that you plan to complete someday: craft projects, fabric to make clothes, photos to put into albums or scrapbooks, things that need to be repaired, magazines you plan to read, recipes you plan to make, and so on.

There are only 24 hours in a day, and after you subtract time to sleep, eat, work, and spend time with family (not necessarily in that order),

there's not much left. Although this may seem
obvious, I see clients every day who are hanging on
to projects they'll never have time to complete. I have
even been guilty of this at times.

It's hard to let go, but I guarantee that you won't
miss these projects when they're gone, and there will
be one less thing for you to do.

◆ If you're having a hard time deciding whether you
can let something go, put it in a box. When the box
is full, tape it up so that it's difficult to get into. Put a "discard or donate"
date on the box for three months from now. When that date arrives, if
you haven't found yourself needing to tear into the box for something,
then it's time to let it go. Resist the urge to open the box again, or you
may find yourself back at square one, wondering if you might need these
things someday. Put the box in the car, and the next time you're out and
about, drop it off.

I guarantee that you won't miss the contents. In all my years of
working with clients, I know of only two instances in which the client
wished they had kept something. Typically people tell me they don't
miss anything they've eliminated, donated, or sold; and most of the
time, they can't even remember what it was that they let go!

6. Group like items together.

As you're sorting and purging, you'll come across possessions you want to keep.
They should be placed in groups of like items. This will make the next two
steps, examining your space and shopping, easier for you. (Yes, you're almost
there—shopping!)

Grouping like items together is the same thing as coming up with categories
of your belongings that will be kept in a particular space in your home. It's
important to complete this step so that you know how many items you have
in each category. That way you can make the best use of your space. When

assigning new "homes" for your things, you want to ensure that you'll have enough space for them in that location. Without grouping them together, this would be challenging to determine. Below are some examples of categories for different rooms in your home. These categories are very basic and will be further discussed in the chapters on each of the rooms.

TIP

Whenever you purchase something new, make a deal with yourself that one or two things you no longer use will leave your home.

Kitchen: pots and pans, baking dishes, small appliances, everyday dishes, glassware, flatware, seasonal dishes, serving pieces, canned goods, boxed goods, storage containers.

Closet: shoes, pants, skirts, dresses, suits, T-shirts, athletic wear, blouses, sweaters, jackets, blazers, gloves, scarves, hats, belts, handbags.

Home office: computer equipment, office supplies, books, filing system, magazines, memorabilia.

Garage: yard tools, sporting gear, tools, extra food and paper products, camping gear, holiday decor, toys, cars. Yes, "cars" is a category for the garage—since many people can't currently park a car in their garage.

7. Examine your space.

As you begin to map out the space in your home for your belongings, you'll need to decide what purpose each space or room will serve. To do this, ask yourself if each space or room works for what it currently holds. Sometimes it becomes necessary to use a space differently. Try to think outside the box for a moment. Don't think about how you've used the space in the past; you are working on a new solution for the future. Oftentimes when I work with new clients in their homes, we reassign rooms or storage areas to fill a different purpose. Think about which items you use most often in the room you're organizing, and make sure that those are the most accessible when you're finished with your organizing project.

Once you decide on the general location for the items you've sorted and grouped into categories, it's time to take a good look at what's left. This will enable you to determine how you'll use the space and what type of products you'll need to invest in to complete your organizing project. Now is the time to start making a list of the products you'll need to help organize and store what you're keeping.

TIP

Get into the habit of going through your home quickly several times a year and gathering things you no longer use or need. Keep a donation box or bag handy, and immediately put those items in it. When the box is full, take it to your favorite thrift shop or other donation location.

Here are a few things to keep in mind before you dash off to the store to shop:

◆ Measure the space you're organizing, and take the measurements with you when you go shopping.

◆ If necessary, draw a diagram of the room on a piece of paper and write the dimensions on it, so that you can show it to whoever helps you at the store.

◆ If you're looking for drawer organizers, measure each drawer individually and make a brief list of what will be kept in each drawer. This will enable you to choose the type of organizer that will best suit your needs.

◆ If you're organizing the garage and have tools to either hang or put into a floor-based organizing unit, you'll want to know how many tools you have. This will enable you to purchase the product that will best suit your needs.

My point is that before you go to the store, you need to have a plan for the space and a good understanding of how much stuff you have to store and organize. This will save you a lot of valuable time and money by enabling you to purchase what you need the first time, so you don't have to make several trips to the store to get things you forgot (because they weren't written down) or exchange things that didn't fit (because you didn't measure).

8. Shop!

Did you think you would never make it to this point? I know that for many people, shopping is the most fun of the 10 steps, so congratulations on resisting the urge to run out to the store and start shopping right away. The reason I wanted you to wait until now to do the shopping is that when you begin any organizing project, you really don't have a good idea of what items will be left to organize until you complete steps 4–6. Had you shopped at the beginning, you might have purchased products that weren't well suited for organizing the items that were left, or for the space you dedicated to those items. Purchasing organizing supplies at the beginning of a project is like putting a square peg into a round hole—it doesn't work. Save yourself the time, money, and frustration by saving the shopping till this phase.

Many of our clients tell us that they have lots of organizing products they've purchased over the years but never used. Why do you think this is? Many times it's because they shopped first and thought something looked like a great idea, but when they got it home, they found that it didn't fit the space or hold what they wanted to organize.

The organizing products industry has become a $10 billion business, offering thousands of solutions to serve just about any need. If you can't find the type of product you're looking for in your local stores, you can always shop online by typing a few keywords into an Internet search engine.

9. Install products.

The second-to-final step is to install any organizing products you've purchased. This can be as easy as placing items in containers and then placing the containers in the area where they'll be kept. Or it can be more time-intensive and complicated if you choose to install a closet system, for example.

TEN STEPS TO ORGANIZING ANY ROOM

Your Quick Reference Guide

1. Dedicate time.

2. Gather supplies.

3. Establish a staging area.

4. Sort.

5. Purge.

6. Group like items together.

7. Examine your space.

8. Shop!

9. Install products and put items into storage containers.

10. Maintain.

THE ORGANIZING PROCESS

13

This is also the point at which you'll be putting into place any remaining items that you're keeping, with or without organizing products. In most cases, you'll probably want to purchase at least a few products to help contain and organize your space.

10. Maintain.

Maintenance is the most important part of any organizing project. Maintenance is something that needs to be done on a regular basis. This could be daily, weekly, biweekly, or monthly, depending on what you've just organized. You need to be the judge of that. Organizing maintenance is no different than going on a diet and then maintaining that new weight. You have to work at it every day, or the weight will come back. If you don't maintain the system in your newly organized space, over time that system will break down, and eventually you may wind up where you started. Here are some examples of maintenance:

Kitchen: If you have organized your kitchen and established a place for everything, maintenance will mean putting the dishes, small appliances, and plastic containers back in their new homes regularly. It will also mean that when you put the groceries away, you put items in their designated areas so that you can keep an accurate inventory, which will ultimately make shopping easier.

Closet: If you've organized your closet and established a place for everything, maintenance will mean continuing to hang each type of clothing in its designated area. It will also mean keeping your shoes in their designated area. Finally, it will mean you won't toss things on the floor that don't belong in the closet.

As you can see, maintenance means different things depending on the area you're organizing and the degree to which things need to be organized. Whether maintaining your new system will take five minutes a day or five hours a week, only you will be able to determine. But maintenance must become part of your routine if you want to live an organized life.

CHAPTER 2

BEATING PROCRASTINATION

Why do today what you can put off until tomorrow? Is that the philosophy of your life? We're all guilty of procrastination, myself included. Of course there are hundreds of reasons why we procrastinate, and just as many excuses to justify our procrastination.

Have you ever stopped to think about why you procrastinate a task that you should be doing? The answer is usually quite simple—we procrastinate because it's much more fun to be doing other activities we enjoy.

Several years ago, I read a book that provided me with a lot of insight into why people procrastinate: *It's About Time!: The 6 Styles of Procrastination and How to Overcome Them*, by Linda Sapadin with Jack Maguire. The authors suggest that there are six styles of procrastination:

1. **The Perfectionist Procrastinator**

2. **The Dreamer Procrastinator**

3. **The Worrier Procrastinator**

4. **The Defier Procrastinator**

5. **The Crisis-Maker Procrastinator**

6. **The Overdoer Procrastinator**

Thanks to their book, I discovered that I am a Perfectionist Procrastinator: I tend to not start things if I can't finish them in a timely fashion to my high level of expectations. This book truly opened my eyes to the idea that not everything I did had to be perfect. The two pieces of wisdom it taught me were:

➤ It's better to finish something that is not quite perfect than to never begin in the first place.

➤ My house doesn't always have to look like a model home.

These two insights had a big impact on me both professionally and personally, and they actually go hand in hand for me these days. What I've learned while running a business is that there isn't enough time in my day for my house to be perfect, and it doesn't have to be.

To answer the question you must be thinking of, yes, my house is organized. It may not always be "picked up"—but there's a difference. I'm asked this question daily, and my answer is always the same. My house is organized: everything has a place, and both cars fit in the garage.

The challenge I have relates to time: I don't always have enough time in my schedule before I go dashing out the door in the morning to put the dishes in the dishwasher or the clothes in the closet, so they lie in the sink or on the couch until I return.

Prior to this revelation, I would never have left the house until everything was completely picked up and put away. Now I've learned to let some of it go till I get home at night. The key here is that I do put things back when I return home, and it's easy because everything has a place.

One of the ways I procrastinate is by putting off tasks I can't complete in a short amount of time. A very good example is a book I started writing three years ago on the subject of organizing one's paperwork. To this date, that book has not been completed. Why? Probably because I thought it would take me too long to complete. I always had better things to do with my time and didn't set a goal to finish it within a certain time frame. I also had no idea how I'd publish it.

The great news is that the sections I did complete are now included in this book, so I'll finally achieve my goal of getting the work published. All it took was a deadline and a plan as to how I was going to accomplish this project. No longer do I procrastinate regarding writing; in fact, I really have learned to enjoy it. It was important for me to step back and look at both my personal and professional life and determine what was holding me back. Now that I've done that, my perspective is quite different.

Dawdling, prolonging, postponing, slacking, and dilly-dallying are just a handful of colorful ways to describe procrastination. Let's face it: putting things off makes you stressed. Here are eight excuses for putting things off, and eight ways to overcome them:

1. I'm easily distracted. Focus is key if you're easily distracted. Keep a to-do list about your project or task at hand. Safeguard yourself from temptation so as not to impede your path to progress.

2. Decisions are overwhelming. Write down a list of pros and cons for the decisions that boggle your mind, and set a deadline to make them.

3. I don't like doing it. If you abhor a task, perhaps a reward for its completion can motivate you to accomplish it. Do you find organizing to be agonizing? Reward yourself with a trip to the store to purchase some fun new products. Remember that shopping is step 8 in our process, so it truly will be your reward for your hard work. If you feel that shopping is just part of the process and an additional reward is necessary, it's OK to treat yourself to something else. Some of our clients treat themselves with a massage or a dinner out. Notice that these rewards are things that won't add any additional clutter to their lives!

4. I'm scared. Perhaps you're a perfectionist and delay starting a task for fear it won't turn out exactly as you imagined. Focus on the process and not the final product. When you disrupt your motivation with unrealistic standards, stop. Take a second look at your reality. Be clear about your expectations, and get to it without worrying about the result. You'll never know until you try!

5. It's too involved. Large, complex projects become more palatable when they're divided into small, manageable tasks. Schedule the toughest elements for your peak energy times, such as first thing in the morning.

6. It's boring. If a project has no benefit for you and seems uninteresting, perhaps you can skip it; perhaps it's not that important after all. Reevaluate the project and drop it unless absolutely necessary. If it's an absolutely necessary task, such as storing dangerous household products out of the reach of children, focus on the necessity and benefit of the job and get to work.

7. "Don't tell me what to do." If a higher-up gives you a project, clarify the expectations and proceed. Try not to think of it as "doing what you're told to do." Focus on the task and the experience you can gain from it. If you're putting off the task for personal reasons, perhaps you're not the right person for the job.

8. It can wait. It's easy to put off today what you can do tomorrow. But tomorrow will never come with that attitude. Assume a proactive approach, and calculate the long-term cost of delay. There's no time like the present!

If you've been procrastinating about organizing a part of your life, a room in your home, or maybe even your entire house, what I want to say to you again is this: There's no time like the present! At the end of this chapter, I'll assign a few action items for you to complete.

This book is designed so that you can turn to certain chapters, read them, and create an action plan. You don't need to read the entire book in order to start organizing a part of your home or life—although of course I do want you to read the entire book at some point!

I guarantee that when you finish organizing an area of your home, you'll feel a great sense of accomplishment, and you'll have proven to yourself that you can do it! You will also feel much more in control of your life, and you won't feel so stressed and overwhelmed.

Please remember, though, this is going to be a process and will take some time—so don't get discouraged. Here is your first assignment:

1. Get a pad of paper and a pen or pencil.

2. Skim the table of contents of this book.

3. Make a list of those areas of your home that you want to organize.

4. Number the list in order of importance.

5. Go through the list again and set yourself a "completion date" for each area of your home. Please remember to be very realistic with yourself here. My goal is for you to succeed. If you put down dates that you can't realistically achieve, you'll feel that you've failed. There's no reason for you to feel this way. Remember, organizing is a process, not an event. Baby steps are the key here.

6. What's the number one priority on your list?

7. Take a new sheet of paper and write this priority at the top.

8. Turn to that chapter in the book.

9. Read the chapter. While you read it, keep your pad of paper close by, and make notes to yourself that will help you complete your goal.

10. When you're finished reading the chapter, you'll be ready to begin your project.

11. Schedule the time for this project on your calendar. Resist the temptation to do anything else except this project on that day. Yes, things will come up, but unless it's an emergency, it doesn't need to bump this event off your calendar. (Events such as going to a movie or lunch with a friend aren't what I consider an emergency, but perhaps those could be your reward for completing your project.)

12. When the day arrives that you've set aside for your project, remember to stay focused on the task at hand. If you have more than one area of your home or life that you want to work on, be sure to schedule time on your calendar for each area. Some projects may require more than one day to complete, so go ahead and schedule multiple days for a project if necessary. Remember to schedule some time to shop for the products you need to complete your project!

The list and calendar you've just created are your "master plan" that contains your goals that you'll achieve. Studies have shown that when goals are written down, there's an 80 percent probability that they'll be reached.

CHAPTER 3

PSYCHOLOGICAL REASONS FOR CLUTTER

Most people don't want their home to look like a used-toy warehouse, but when it comes down to getting rid of the clutter, they just can't seem to let go. Why is it that we cling to items of no apparent value or things that we know are junk? In this chapter I'll discuss five reasons why people hang on to these things: depression, denial, grief, thrift, and cluttered upbringing.

DEPRESSION

Depression is caused by an imbalance of the chemicals in your brain. Despite what many believe, depression isn't something you can just "snap out of." It affects people in different ways. Loss of a loved one, divorce, and the end of a long-term relationship are three of the leading causes of depression in clients I've worked with.

People who suffer from depression have different ways of coping with it. Many of my clients cope with depression by shopping. I like to refer to this coping mechanism as "retail therapy." In a way, retail therapy becomes their "drug of choice." Other depressed people may turn to alcohol or food. Some may be receiving medical treatment or counseling, and some may not be getting treated at all.

We have all probably succumbed to retail therapy at some point in our lives; after all, most people (especially women) like to shop and to treat themselves. But retail therapy associated with depression is much more extreme than the occasional trip to the mall to purchase a new pair of shoes, a fun new handbag, an outfit that makes you feel great, or the latest electronic gadget that you just can't live without.

With depressed people, retail therapy manifests itself like this: You walk into a bedroom that's completely filled with shopping bags crammed with all sorts of treasures. There's a path that leads to the bed and maybe one to the closet—if you're lucky. The bags are stacked on top of each other with no rhyme or reason, and it's impossible to know where anything is or what's even in the bags. Due to the sheer volume of items, many depressed people don't remember what they've purchased until they see it again, and even then they may not recall the purchase.

The reason I call retail therapy the drug of choice for some people who suffer from depression is that they get a temporary "high" from making a purchase. However, it's usually *very* temporary: their homes are often full of so many other things they've purchased in this fashion that once they get the new purchases home, the items simply stay in their bags, never to see the light of day again.

As I work with individuals, I gradually find out a lot of personal information about them, which helps me put some of the puzzle pieces in place. So many times this "retail therapy" has started in large part because of the loss of a loved one or a divorce. Shopping becomes their way of coping with the situation.

> **Solution:** I'm not an expert on depression, but I've learned from my real-life education and experience of working with clients who suffer from this disease. I believe it's important to seek professional help in treating depression. A professional can help determine why a person has developed this behavior as a coping mechanism. With a willingness to accept help and a desire to change, individuals can overcome such behavior patterns.

> **True story:** Several years ago, we worked with a client who owned several homes in different parts of the country. The home we worked in was about 9,000 square feet. Most of the rooms, including the three-car garage, were filled with things the client didn't know she owned. In fact, she kept the doors shut to many of the rooms because there was so much stuff in them. When she needed something, because it was almost impossible to find anything, she would go out and purchase another one—resulting in even more clutter.

After working with her for several sessions, we got to talking about the past. I already knew that she had suffered the loss of a child many years earlier, and

I suspected that some of the shopping was a way of coping with that loss. During our conversation, I found out that my client had once been very well organized and shopped only when she needed something, not just because she wanted something. After her son passed away, though, she found it extremely difficult to be at home without her, and so she began to shop. And shop she did, for more than 10 years, until the entire house was full.

Time and again I've seen this scenario played out. Whether it's a child, a parent, or a spouse who is no longer present, it is a loss, and many fill the void with shopping.

DENIAL

How many of us hold on to old clothing because we believe that we'll one day wear it again? Many people hang on to outfits that are the wrong size or from a different era. What we don't realize is that these items of clothing, to which we cling so dearly, won't be in style by the time they fit again. In the end, they just take up valuable space in our closets, making it difficult to see the items we do wear regularly.

Solution: Donate or toss clothes that don't fit you or haven't been worn in the last year. If you need some sort of motivation for dieting, save one pair of "skinny pants." Special-occasion items can be kept for more than a year—but try to keep in mind that they'll go out of style and you'll want something new to wear anyway.

True story: During the past five years, I've helped a number of women organize their closets. Several of these projects took place because there were simply too many clothes and other things in the closet, making it impossible to find anything, make room for anything new, or put back what they had worn.

Since we typically wear only about 20 percent of what we own on a regular basis, you can imagine that there are a lot of clothes in closets that haven't seen the light of day in years. I've personally seen several closets containing an astronomical amount of clothing from the 1980s! And I know for a fact that these clothes had not been worn in a long time, because they were covered in dust.

Most of these clothes are kept because "I might fit back into it someday" or "It might come back in style someday." The old adage "Someday never comes" certainly applies here. In a couple of instances, I've played fashion police with some of our clients. They'll try on the clothes, and after several outfit changes, without even asking for my opinion or looking at the expression on my face, they begin to realize how silly they've been. The clothes start coming out of the closet and going into bags to be donated or tossed.

I can think of two "closet clients" in particular who filled at least 20 giant black garbage bags with clothes to be donated, all things they had not worn in many years! After we were done purging all of the outdated, never-worn, and wrong-size clothing, we could then begin to organize the rest of the clothing. Yes, there were still clothes left after the purge!

In all of these instances, I know that it was a very freeing experience for the clients to be able to let go of the clothing. They were finally able to see what they had to wear, and they were also able to get a better feel for what pieces of clothing they actually needed to shop for.

I'm happy to report that I've never had anyone call me later because they missed a certain piece of clothing that was donated. In fact, most say they don't even know what was given away, and many even discover a few items they'd forgotten they had. (For ideas on how to organize your closet, see chapter 5.)

GRIEVING

A very common reason for clinging to "things" is that those things remind us of someone who is no longer in our life. We save souvenirs from trips we took with ex-partners, deceased spouses, or relatives who have passed on. Why do we hold on to these items so tenaciously? Part of the answer is that they hold precious memories and provide a link to the past. We project memories onto those objects. The other part of the answer is that we're still in the process of grieving.

Solution: There are a few things that can help us facilitate the grieving process and encourage organization and healthy living. First, we can remind ourselves that the meaning is in the memory, not the memorabilia. Second, we can slowly begin the purging process, keeping some very special treasures while eliminating others. Begin by going through just a few things at a time. Allow yourself to relive the memory, but agree that not everything associated with the memory needs to be kept. Do this every so often, until the number of treasures you're keeping is manageable. Lastly, we can simply move old memorabilia into storage until we feel emotionally able to deal with it. Removing the memorabilia from our everyday lives is a good way of facilitating healing and letting go.

True story: In 2001 my grandpa passed away at the age of 91. Several months after his passing, my uncle Bill took photos of many of Grandpa's possessions and mounted them on poster board, along with a description of each item. (Can you say "organized"? I think it runs in the family.) Anyway, one day my aunt Jean came to my house with the poster boards showing all the items we were to divide up among the grandchildren and my mom's brothers and sister. After looking at the photos, I told my aunt that I didn't want any of the items. She looked at me puzzledly.

I explained that every day I work with clients to help them let go of things that don't bring them joy or serve a purpose in their lives. Sure, these things had belonged to my grandpa, but they didn't mean anything to me and didn't hold any special memories. That's because during the 25 or 30 years that I visited my grandparents, I never saw those items displayed in their home, because they were packed away in boxes in my grandpa's closet. Had the items been out in the open when I visited, I may have felt differently about some of them. In the end, I didn't take anything. The memories of my grandpa that I wanted to keep, I already had, in the photos that I had taken over the years. I can honestly say that four years later, I don't regret not having any of those items.

THRIFT

Many people refuse to throw something out because they believe that it will be useful again someday. This is especially true with things that can potentially be turned into art or home-improvement projects, such as old, outdated fabrics, furniture, and other craft supplies. It's perfectly fine to save a few things in hopes of someday recycling them. Problems arise, however, when we feel compelled to save everything. In most homes, there simply isn't room to hold on to everything.

Solution: There are a few things you can do to minimize this kind of clutter. First, keep one storage box that you designate for future crafts. Second, if you can't think of something specific you want to do with an item, throw it out immediately. Trust me, it will never be used; it will only collect dust and take up space. Lastly, if you don't use the item in three months, donate it. We often have good intentions but nothing to show for them except a drawer, closet, or basement filled with useless clutter.

True story: Several years ago, we worked with a client on what turned out to be one of our largest projects ever. The client's new home was four full stories. In the basement of the home was a large room dedicated to gift wrapping. It contained enough gift-wrapping supplies to start a small store.

One day while organizing the client's bedroom, I found a dusty, smashed bow. I threw it in the garbage. Typically, it's my policy to ask before throwing items away; however, in this case, I figured it would be OK since it looked old and wasn't in any shape to be reused. Also, because there were a few hundred more bows in the basement, I felt it would be a better use of my time to throw it out rather than to walk down two flights of stairs to put it in the gift-wrapping room.

As you may have guessed, I assumed incorrectly. When I arrived at the client's home the next day, I was informed that I should not have thrown the bow away. After a half-hour discussion on this matter, I took the bow, which the client had retrieved from the trash, and placed it in its home in the gift-wrapping room.

You might be chuckling to yourself at this moment, but this story is a good example of an extreme case of thrift. This client grew up during the Depression era; if you're familiar with those times, then you'll know why this bow was saved.

As you begin to make decisions about items you have been saving, please keep this story in mind. If this dusty, smashed bow had been yours, would you ever have used it on a package? Chances are a prettier, crisp, clean bow would have been used every time, meaning that the smashed, dusty bow would just continue to take up space.

If you suffer from an extreme case of thrift, it's important to take a step back and do a brief reality check about the condition of the items you're saving, as well as the likelihood that you'll ever reuse them.

CLUTTERED UPBRINGING

Perhaps you grew up in a cluttered home, so that's the type of lifestyle you're accustomed to. Children learn by example. If you were raised in a home without systems or designated areas for items, then chances are your own home resembles that one. Similarly, if your children are currently living in a cluttered environment, you can't expect them to clean up their act until you've cleaned up yours.

> **Solution:** The good news is that you can choose not to live in this type of environment anymore. Just because you were raised in a messy home doesn't mean that your own home needs to be messy too. As a child, it's easy to have excuses for why your environment is cluttered—after all, you just live there, right? But as an adult, you really don't have an excuse—you have the ability to create the environment and lifestyle you want.

> **True story:** I recently helped a client named Karen organize her home. Karen had gotten a brochure of mine a couple of years ago and kept thinking she should call. One day after she had lost her keys and misplaced a credit card, she rediscovered my brochure, which she had stuffed into a drawer. She decided that it must be time to call and get a bit of organizing assistance.

When Karen and I initially spoke, she told me that she had grown up in a home where things didn't have a place and there were no systems for her to follow. Because of this, she said, "I don't know how to organize my own home." Now that her daughter was getting ready to begin first grade, she wanted to set a good example for her.

Karen's goals in this process were as follows:

➤ To create a place for her daughter's toys, crafts, and school supplies so that it would be easy for her to complete homework on a daily basis.

Karen wanted her daughter to be able to find things quickly, when she needed them, without having to search the house.

◆ To create a home environment that her husband was proud to live in, since he had been accustomed to living in an organized home.

◆ To establish a place for all of her things and stop stuffing items in drawers or closets or dropping them on the floor.

The first day Karen and I met, we sat at her kitchen table and discussed her prioritized list of areas that she wanted to organize. I could see that this was a very emotional process for Karen, as there were tears in her eyes. It was a huge step for her to admit that she needed help and was ready to make a lifestyle change. She knew that she no longer wanted to live the way she had been raised, but she wasn't sure where to start or how to get to a better place.

Working together, Karen and I used my 10-step process in several rooms of her home. We started out with some relatively simple projects on some junk drawers in the kitchen and gradually made our way through closets, bathrooms, family living areas, and the basement. Although some of the projects we did could be considered small, such as the junk drawers in the kitchen, they made a huge impact because they enabled family members to quickly find things like writing instruments, scissors, candles, matches, and tools, just to name a few.

I'm happy to say that Karen and her family now live in an organized home, and she is able to maintain the systems that we created together. I'm so proud of Karen for recognizing that she didn't need to continue living her life the way she grew up, and for working hard to reach all of her goals!

These are only a few of the reasons people hang on to clutter; there are surely many more. I encourage you to look at what you're holding on to and decide whether it's truly a cherished treasure or just "stuff."

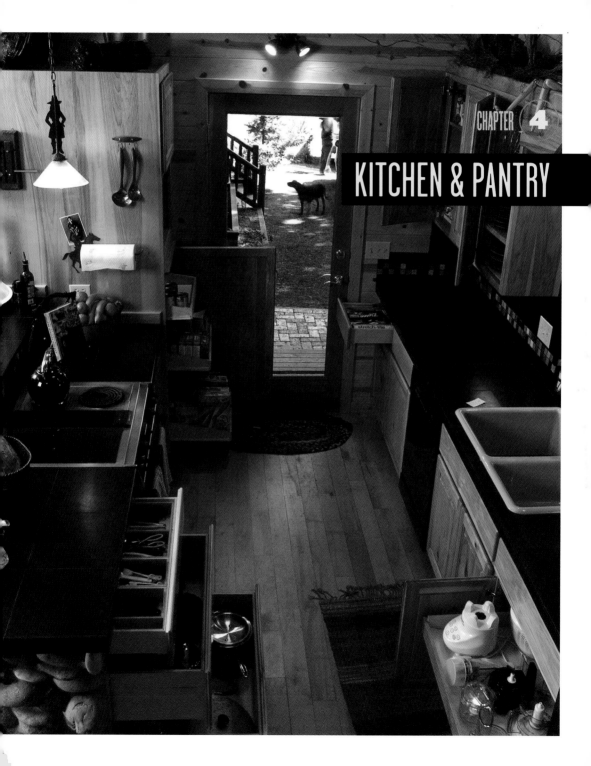

CHAPTER 4

KITCHEN & PANTRY

Have you ever noticed that the kitchen is the central meeting place of your home? Most families use their kitchens two or three times a day, yet the kitchen is often one of the least efficiently organized rooms in the home. The last time you entertained, did you notice how everyone congregated in the kitchen? Did you get just a little bit nervous wondering if someone was going to open one of your cupboards, sending everything inside crashing to the floor? Maybe you had heart palpitations just thinking about what you would say if someone opened your pantry!

Cynthia and Ron Dotzauer used to have these same fears when they entertained, but not anymore.

The first time I saw Cynthia and Ron's kitchen was when I peered through the windows of their beautiful log home in Snohomish, Washington. Their home has a Western theme and is warm, welcoming, and charming. I'd been invited to their "Round-Up at the Ranch," an annual event held outdoors on their property. I always like to see how people have decorated their homes, which is why I could be found with my nose pressed up against the windows.

Several months later, Cynthia contacted me about helping her organize her home. I thought she must be kidding because during my entire time at the Round-Up, I didn't see one thing out of place! She then confessed that before the event, she had scooped things up, put them in bins, or shoved them behind closed doors so that no one would see her clutter.

When I did a walk-through of her home, I offered many suggestions for using products to better organize what she had and for making better use of the space. Cynthia was game for doing much of the organizing on her own after sorting, purging, and then purchasing many of the products I recommended. But she had already decided that the kitchen was too much to tackle on her own. For that room, she needed our help.

PROJECT BREAKDOWN

TOTAL HOURS (24)

TASK	HOURS
Sorting, purging, and organizing	18.5
Cynthia's shopping and installation time	1
Laura's shopping time	1.5
Installation time for pull-out shelves	1
Hauling away donations	1
Cleanup	1
Total project time	**24 HOURS**

Cynthia allowed me to open the cupboards, drawers, and pantry and take a peek inside. What I saw was pretty typical: lots of stuff that's never used, shoved in places where it can't be found or isn't easily accessible. No problem, I thought to myself—nothing that a day of organizing can't cure!

The more I thought about it after I left, the more I realized that Cynthia and Ron's kitchen was the perfect one for this book. It's representative of the problems many homeowners face every day in their kitchens: too much stuff that isn't easily accessible. I asked Cynthia if we could feature her kitchen in this book, and I was so excited when she said yes!

I encouraged Cynthia to do two things before we began work on her kitchen:

◆ Eat as much of the food as possible in the cupboards and pantry that had been on hand for a while (and was still OK to eat).

◆ Eliminate anything that no longer had a use or purpose in her kitchen.

Cynthia successfully completed her homework assignment (with the help of other family members, who enthusiastically assisted with the first item!), and we were ready to begin her project.

Having a well laid-out and efficient kitchen can mean the difference between enjoying meal preparation and dreading it. Here are the steps we took to organize Cynthia and Ron's kitchen.

THE PROCESS

1. Dedicate time.

The kitchen is one of the most time-consuming spaces in your home to keep organized and clean. You may want to set aside an entire day to devote to this project, if you plan to conquer a kitchen similar to Cynthia's. You want to make sure that once you tear apart the contents of your cupboards, drawers, and pantry, you have enough time to complete the project and get everything put back.

If you're unable to dedicate this much time to your kitchen, consider dividing the task into smaller pieces and going through a few cupboards or drawers each day instead, to eliminate anything you're no longer using. You can immediately put back the items you want to keep, and then organize the remaining items in the kitchen at a later date. This is step 4 (sort); we'll discuss it in more detail in the pages to follow.

Cynthia did exactly this: she went through each cupboard and drawer and eliminated anything she wasn't using or didn't like. She then immediately put the rest of the items back into their respective areas until we could meet to organize her kitchen. She was pretty shocked by the amount of "stuff" she was able to let go of that she hadn't used in years, and she didn't even miss it once it was gone.

2. Gather supplies.

The supplies we gathered for Cynthia and Ron's kitchen organizing project were pretty minimal: garbage bags (and plenty of them!) and plastic storage containers. You may also want an old sheet or some card tables.

3. Establish a staging area.

We used several areas of the kitchen and dining room as staging areas—places to put everything we removed from the cupboards and drawers. These areas included the kitchen counters, the kitchen floor, and the dining room table. Although we used the floor, we didn't set items directly on it; rather, we used plastic storage containers to group similar items together, such as canned goods, baking supplies, beverages, boxed foods, and so on (as you'll notice in corresponding photo 6).

You may wish to lay down an old sheet or blanket so you don't have to put items directly on the floor. If you don't like the idea of bending over all day, you may want to use card tables instead.

4. Sort.

As discussed in step 1, we divided the sorting among several different time periods, partly because Cynthia had a very limited amount of time to work on this project.

How you go about sorting depends on how much stuff you have in your kitchen. With some clients, I recommend emptying all of the cupboards and drawers, just as you would do if you were moving. But if you can already see all the contents of each drawer or cupboard, you don't need to empty them entirely. Remember, organizing isn't an exercise in shuffling or moving things around in your cupboards to make them look neat and tidy. It's about creating a functional work space where you can quickly and easily locate those items you need on a regular basis.

In Cynthia and Ron's kitchen, we completely emptied about half of the drawers and cupboards. Notice in photo 4 how Kari, one of the Eliminate Chaos consultants, is removing the food from the cupboards and pantry, as well as from a few random pull-out shelves where we found food items. These are the items

FOUR COMMON PROBLEMS OF KITCHENS

1. Space is used inefficiently.

2. Food is wasted because you don't know what you have, either because there's too much or because you can't see all of it.

3. The kitchen has become an appliance junkyard—you have too many appliances that are never used but are taking up valuable space.

4. Lots of mismatched and chipped dishes, glassware, and coffee mugs are taking up space but not being used.

❶

❶ Cynthia and Ron's kitchen before we got to work.

❷ The pantry, with just two pull-out shelves and a lot of wasted space between each shelf. The roll of paper towels, the tallest item on the bottom shelf, was moved to another location so we didn't need to plan for that tall of a space on the bottom pull-out shelf.

❸ Cynthia's cupboard before the organizing makeover. Although Cynthia was using two can risers, she still had trouble finding what she needed and didn't always know what she had on hand, so duplicate items were sometimes purchased.

❹

②

③

⑥

⑤

④ Kari removes items from the cupboards and places them in our staging area, where she will group like items together.

⑤ Some of the spatulas I removed from Cynthia and Ron's drawers—there were too many for me to hold!

⑥ Plastic bins used to remove items from cupboards. These were then sorted into groups of like items.

7

8

10

7 Kari carefully measures and cuts our Cushy Cupboards shelf liner for the cupboards, drawers, and pull-out shelves.

8 A new shelf was cut for the cupboard to house the glasses and mugs to allow for additional storage, instead of double-stacking glasses. Here, Cynthia and I get ready to set the new shelf in place.

9 After spices were removed from this drawer, it freed up a lot of space for the utensils, which are now beautifully organized into wood drawer organizers, with items grouped together so they're easily located.

9

11

10 The drawer was emptied of items that were not used every day—such as batteries and tools—which were moved to another location in the house. Items such as food wrap and storage bags—which are used every day—we placed in the drawer instead.

Two turntables were placed on the middle shelf to hold cooking oils, vinegars, and peanut butter—thus giving quick and easy access to frequently used items.

An expandable can riser was used to hold canned soups, fruits, and vegetables—making it very easy to see each can. We divided the can riser into sections to hold each type of canned good.

On the top shelf, we placed a plastic bin on the right side that contained all of the baking supplies, making it easy to pull them all down at once when baking.

On the bottom pull-out shelf, we placed a plastic bin to hold the onions and garlic in place. This also helped to keep the pull-out shelf free of peels that flake off the onions.

Sugar, brown sugar, and nuts were placed in plastic containers on the bottom pull-out shelf. These containers are lightweight and see-through, and can be run through the dishwasher.

A new turning spice rack was used to free up valuable drawer space.

11 The new and improved pantry with three pull-out shelves. Each pull-out was strategically placed at a height that would allow for storage of cereals, boxed pastas, and canned goods.

that we sorted by category into our plastic storage containers on the floor. The categories we developed were cereal and other breakfast food, seasonings and spices, baking items, boxed food (rice, pasta, couscous), canned goods, beverages (tea, coffee, drink mixes), and snacks (chips, raisins, nuts).

I had earlier suggested that Cynthia start using up the existing food in the cupboards and pantry so that she could see what she really had on hand, which in turn would help her plan better for grocery shopping. Many times people purchase food because they have no idea what's in the cupboard at home—they simply can't see what's there.

Because Cynthia did such a great job with her homework, she didn't have a lot of food that needed to be tossed. There were two main categories that we did pare down: teas and spices. We tossed those that were no longer being used and were no longer fresh. (See the "Kitchen Organizing Tips" section at the end of this chapter for information on tea and spice storage and shelf life.)

We had Cynthia go through the rest of her cupboards and drawers and determine whether each item was something that should be donated, tossed, or kept. We also had Cynthia tell us which items she used most often, so we would be sure to place them in a convenient-to-reach location.

5. Purge.

As mentioned in step 4, although Cynthia had previously gone through her cupboards and purged many items on her own, she did a second round of elimination the day we were there. It was amazing to see how much more stuff she let go of in a very short amount of time. When we were done, we had six 30-gallon trash bags full of donations and three bags of trash.

As you look at the contents of your kitchen, be honest with yourself and ask, "When was the last time I used this item?" You may also wish to ask yourself the following:

➤ How many mismatched coffee cups and mugs are in your cupboards? How many do you really use?

◆ How many plastic containers do you really need? How many of these don't have matching tops or bottoms? With those that don't, it's time to do some tossing.

◆ How many of your spatulas look as if the garbage disposal ate them for lunch? How many can you cook with at one time? Notice in photo 5 how many spatulas we pulled out of Cynthia and Ron's kitchen drawers.

◆ How many kitchen appliances do you own that you never or rarely use, but are taking up valuable space in your kitchen?

6. Group like items together.

While we were sorting and purging, we started to group like items together so that we could see how how many items of each type Cynthia had. This would enable us to determine how to best use the space and what we needed to shop for. Notice in photo 6 how we have the canned goods, paper products, tea, pasta, oils and seasonings, peanut butter, jelly, and honey grouped together on the floor in plastic containers.

The categories of items we came up with for Cynthia and Ron's kitchen consisted of the following: vases, paper products, glasses, coffee mugs, tea and accompanying items, small appliances, plastic containers, kitchen towels, pot-holders, aprons, pots and pans, silverware, cooking utensils, plates and bowls, snack foods, cereal, baking goods, baking dishes and mixing bowls, serving pieces, canned goods, spices and seasonings, serving pitchers, beverages (tea, coffee, hot chocolate), cleaning supplies, and food wrap.

It's important to group like items together because as you start to map out where everything will be kept, you'll want to see how much you have in each category. Due to space limitations, you may end up not storing everything together that you grouped together. This was certainly the case in Cynthia and Ron's kitchen, as I'll explain in step 7, examining your space, and step 9, installing products.

As you look at what you currently have stored in your kitchen, you'll most likely find that you have the following groups of items: everyday dishes, glasses and mugs, utensils, pots and pans, small appliances, bakeware, mixing bowls, and plastic containers or Tupperware.

7. Examine your space.

After we completed the above steps, most of Cynthia's cupboards and drawers were fairly empty, so we were able to start figuring out how we would like to use the space to create homes for everything. There were three areas in Cynthia and Ron's kitchen that we needed to modify in order to create additional space: the pantry; the cupboard containing the glasses, mugs, tea, and honey; and the drawer containing tools, batteries, and the like (which needed to be removed).

In the pantry, Cynthia already had two pull-out shelves (photo 2), but there was a lot of wasted space between the shelves. We determined that we should have three pull-out shelves instead (photo 11). Because of the way the original two shelves were installed, we would need to remove them and replace them with three new ones.

One of the very narrow kitchen cupboards above the counter held the glasses and mugs that were used every day. Although the cupboard was very narrow, it was also quite tall. Given the number of glasses and mugs that needed to be kept in this cupboard, and the fact that we didn't want them to be stacked on top of one another, we determined that the best solution was to cut a piece of wood and create an additional shelf in that cupboard (photo 8).

We also wanted to be able to store the tea and honey alongside the mugs so that Ron would not have to take so many steps in the kitchen in order to make his tea every morning. We decided to store these items in the cupboard right above the sink area, where the instant hot water was located.

The final area that needed to be modified was a drawer full of batteries, tools, and miscellaneous items. We needed extra drawer space, and using an entire drawer just for batteries seemed like a poor use of space, so we put the batteries and tools in the laundry room instead. We now had an entire empty drawer for the sandwich bags, aluminum foil, and plastic wrap (photo 10). In the past, these items had been stored in various different drawers.

After thinking about how we could maximize the use of space in the kitchen, we concluded that we also needed to do the following:

◆ Move some of the existing shelves up or down. It really is amazing to see how much more stuff you can fit into a cupboard when you move the shelves around to best fit the contents. In most homes, the shelves are adjustable.

◆ Purchase several products that would help us contain the items we wanted to keep together.

Here are some ideas to get you started thinking about how specific organizing products can help you maximize the use of space in your kitchen:

◆ Install pull-out shelves or drawers.

◆ Use turntables.

◆ Use can risers for canned goods.

◆ Install racks for canned goods on the inside of pantry doors.

◆ Use a freestanding cabinet in a utility room or garage for kitchen overflow—such as infrequently used appliances, items used when entertaining, or extra bulk food and paper products.

◆ Install a hanging rack for pots and pans.

8. Shop!

Before you go dashing off to the store, do the following:

◆ Create a list of the groups of items you want to organize. You may even want to indicate the specific number of each item you need to store, such as "32 spices" or "12 bottles of oil, vinegar, and other condiments."

◆ Measure. Need I say more? Take the measurements with you. You'll thank yourself later when you don't have to go back to the store to return something because it doesn't fit.

◆ Take photos of your space or items to be stored, so you can show them to the clerks at the store as you describe what you want to accomplish. (This will be especially easy with a digital camera.)

With all these items in hand, it's time to shop! The list on page 45 shows what we bought.

9. Install products.

When you're ready to start putting things back in their new locations in the kitchen, and installing the products to hold them, consider establishing a location for those items you use most frequently first, such as dishes, glasses, and utensils. If possible, place them near the dishwasher so you don't have to take so many steps to put most of them away.

Items you don't often use should be placed on the top shelves or at the back of the bottom shelves—in an out-of-the-way location, but still easy to access when the time arises. For example, if you have a waffle maker that you use twice a year, store it at the back of a shelf instead of in front, where it would take up space that could better be filled by something you use more frequently.

Installing products can mean one of two things: either physically installing them, such as the pull-out shelves for Cynthia, or placing them in their new location and filling them with the items they were intended to organize, such as spices or teas. Be sure to wipe down shelves and drawers before you start installing products or putting things away.

Here's how we used the products in Cynthia and Ron's kitchen:

Plastic bin (shoebox size): This bin was used to contain dish towels on one of the pull-out shelves next to the kitchen sink. Cynthia didn't have enough towel drawers close to the sink, but the cabinet to the right of

PRODUCT LIST

STORE	ITEM/SERVICE	SIZE	COST	TOTAL $
Pull-Outs Plus	Pull-out shelves	Each pull-out shelf is custom built to maximize access to space in existing shelves and open storage spaces.	3 × 69.00–89.00	267.00
	Installation			75.00
			total	342.00
Cushy Cupboards	Shelf liner for upper cupboards	12" × 10'	2 × 12.00	24.00
	Shelf liner for lower cupboards	24" × 10'	2 × 19.00	38.00
			total	62.00
Other Stores	Plastic bin	shoebox size 8⅛" W × 13⁹⁄₁₆" D × 4⁵⁄₁₆" H		1.50
	Plastic bins	small 10¾" W × 16³⁄₁₆" D × 5⅞" H	4 × 2.50	10.00
	Plastic bin	square 13¾" W × 16³⁄₁₆" D × 7⅛" H		4.00
	Acrylic tea box			11.95
	Microwave lid			2.50
	Plastic canisters	small	3 × 3.95	11.85
	Plastic canisters	large	2 × 4.95	9.90
	Plastic bins without lids		3 × 2.95	8.85
	Turntables (brushed metal)		2 × 10.95	21.90
	Spice rack (chrome)			39.95
	Utensil drawer insert	large		16.95
	Utensil drawer inserts	small	4 × 5.95	23.80
			total	163.15
Tupperware	Seasoning packet holder			19.00
			TOTAL COST OF KITCHEN PRODUCTS	$586.15

the sink had plenty of room on the bottom. We used the plastic bin to hold them all in place.

Plastic bins (small): One of the four bins was used to store baking supplies, such as food coloring, cupcake tins, vanilla, baking powder, baking soda, and birthday candles. Another was placed on the top shelf in the cupboard with the canned goods to contain the seasonings and spices (photo 3). It's perfect for the top shelf because it allows you to pull everything down all at once instead of shoving individual items on the top shelf, never to be seen again.

The third small bin was used to store small snack food items such as protein bars, and was placed on one of the pull-out shelves in the pantry. Finally, we used a fourth bin to store and contain the onions and garlic, and placed it on the bottom pull-out shelf below the counter.

Acrylic tea box: This box was used for storing teabags. The tea box we chose has six compartments, which gave Ron a good variety of tea to select from each morning. As mentioned previously, the tea box was placed in the cupboard with the honey and the mugs, so that everything he needed to make his tea was in one place and quick to grab. The extra teabags that wouldn't fit in the organizer were kept in their boxes in a larger plastic bin, so they could be taken out all at one time to refill the tea box.

Microwave lid: A microwave lid is used to cover a plate or bowl when reheating food in the microwave. It eliminates having to clean the microwave because a meal exploded or splattered. Instead, you just toss the lid in the dishwasher when it gets dirty. It's best to keep the lid in the microwave when not in use; that way, in order to heat something, you have to remove the lid first, which means you won't forget to place the lid over your dish.

Plastic canisters (small): The canisters were used to store sugar, brown sugar, and nuts on the bottom pull-out shelf in the cabinet below the counter. That shelf contained some of the baking dishes as well.

Plastic canisters (large): These canisters were used for flour and sugar and were placed on the same pull-out shelf, directly behind the three smaller canisters (photo 10).

Turntables: The two turntables were used for some of the canned goods in Cynthia's cupboard. One was used for peanut butter, jelly, honey, Karo syrup, and molasses. The other one was used for oils, vinegar, and other seasonings and dressings.

You'll notice in photo 3 that the cabinet with the canned goods, oils, and teas looks fairly organized. After all, Cynthia did have can risers already in place. Notice, though, that at the end of each can riser on the shelf, there are a lot of oils and other bottles that are difficult to see because one bottle is placed in front of the next. Using the turntables (photo 10) allows Cynthia to see everything that she has while still taking up the same amount of space.

Spice rack: This is one of my favorite parts of Cynthia and Ron's kitchen now, for several reasons. One of the challenges in this kitchen is that there is limited drawer space. Originally the spices had been placed in a drawer, where they took up a lot of that valuable space. Because of this, Cynthia had her cooking utensils spread throughout five other locations. Our goal was to get all the utensils in the same drawer, the one to the left of the stove, for quick and easy access. We were able to do this by moving the spices to the new standing spice rack and using wood drawer dividers for her utensils.

The spice rack we chose holds 24 spices and fits perfectly on the shelf next to the two turntables. Notice the height of the spice rack in relation to the items on the turntables in photo 10. Placing these three items together on one shelf allowed us to further maximize the use of space in that cupboard.

Utensil drawer insert (large): The utensil drawer was quite wide, so we were able to use one insert to hold spoons, spatulas, and a few other various items (photo 9).

Utensil drawer inserts (small): We still had extra space in the drawer and several smaller items to contain. We used four smaller wood drawer inserts that now hold items such as the measuring cups, potato peelers and garlic press, measuring spoons, and pizza slicer, to name just a few. You can see in photo 9 how well we were able to fill up the drawer with different organizers because we had measured the drawer and knew what we needed to store in it.

10. Maintain.

With a newly organized kitchen and a much better use of their space, Cynthia and Ron now have a very easy-to-maintain kitchen. A kitchen is an area of the home that you'll want to maintain on a daily basis—which means putting the dishes back in the same location after they've been used and, of course, washed! After you've shopped for groceries, the idea is the same; put them away, in their assigned locations, right after you come home. Finally, at least once or twice a year, take a quick pass through your drawers and cupboards to purge items you're no longer using.

I'm happy to report that even I practice this exercise at least twice a year, if not more often. It seems as if every time I either give a talk on kitchen organization or write about it, I'm inspired to go through my drawers and cupboards and eliminate things I'm no longer using. On my last pass through my kitchen, I filled an entire large box with items I never use.

KITCHEN ORGANIZING TIPS

I f reading about Cynthia and Ron's kitchen inspired you, here are some more tips to help you organize your own kitchen:

1. Line shelves and drawers. Liners protect not only the items you put on the shelves or in the drawers, but also the drawers and shelves themselves. We lined most of Cynthia's drawers and shelves where she would be moving items in and out on a regular basis. You don't need to use liners if there are turntables or drawer inserts, though, because those shelves and drawers are already protected.

2. Establish a junk drawer. It's perfectly acceptable to have a junk drawer in your kitchen—I even have one in mine! The idea is to not have it look junky. There are plenty of drawer organizers available that will suit your needs perfectly. Be sure to measure your drawer first to find the best fit, and have a good idea of what you plan to store in it so you can get an organizer with the right number of compartments. Many drawer organizers have moveable parts so you can adjust the compartments to be the size you want.

When organizing your junk drawer, dump the contents on the counter, sort them, toss what you no longer need, and put misplaced things in the locations where they should be. Then you can organize the rest of what's left to be stored in the drawer.

3. Fix broken appliances. If you need a part for one of your small appliances, Culinary Parts Unlimited is one place to try. Visit www.culinaryparts.com or call 866-PART-HELP.

4. Remember that most shelves are adjustable. In my five years as an organizing consultant, there have been only a handful of occasions when I wasn't able to adjust a shelf to create more space. Many times you can also have an additional shelf cut for your cupboards if you need more shelf space.

This is what we did in Cynthia and Ron's kitchen (photo 8). Their very narrow cupboard, used for glasses and coffee mugs, would not hold them all unless they were stacked, so we cut an additional shelf and drilled a few more holes in the side for pegs for the shelf to sit on.

Where you can, try to group things together that are approximately the same height to maximize use of the space. Shelves should be adjusted so that the shelf above the tallest item on the shelf below allows you just enough space to move items in and out of the cupboards easily.

5. Use turntables. Turntables are a great organizing tool for a variety of items. I particularly like to use them for spices, oils, and vinegars in cupboards. It keeps these items from getting shoved into the back of the cupboard, making it difficult to see what you have. I also like to put turntables in corner cabinets that are above the counter. This is an excellent place to store spices, oils, and vinegars, typically on the two lowest shelves (photo 10).

You can put one large turntable on each shelf or use two side by side. I find that to maximize the space in this area, it's best to use one large turntable on the bottom shelf for larger jars such as oil, vinegars, honey, peanut butter, large spices, and sauces. Above that shelf is a great place to put two smaller turntables for your spices.

Don't worry that you can't see the contents of the entire turntable—that's the beauty of the product. You don't need to see everything at once because you can spin it around and get to what you need. It's more important to make use of as much space in this corner area, and two 9-inch or 10-inch side-by-side turntables are often the perfect solution.

We also used a very large turntable—21 inches in diameter—on the top shelf of the pantry (photo 11). Because this shelf is high and deep, the turntable makes it much easier to access items such as pitchers, the iced tea maker, and spaghetti than if they were just on the shelf.

6. Discard old spices and seasonings. Here are some general guidelines for how long they can be kept:

> **Herbs:** 1–3 years
>
> **Seasoning blends and mixes:** 1–2 years
>
> **Ground spices:** 3 years
>
> **Seeds:** 4 years, except for poppy seeds and sesame seeds, which should be kept for no more than 2 years
>
> **Whole spices:** 4 years

You can also use a simple "sniff" test to see if they still smell fresh—if they don't, it's time to toss them. Spices should be stored in a cool, dark, dry location in airtight containers to maintain optimum freshness. It's not a good idea to store spices and herbs on the kitchen counter (because of the light) or above the stove or next to the dishwasher (because of the heat). This was another good reason to move the spices in Cynthia and Ron's kitchen: they had previously been stored in a drawer to the left of the oven and stove. A good way to remember when you should eliminate the spices is to put a "toss" date on the bottom or top of the jar that's one year from the date you opened it.

7. Alphabetize your spices. Alphabetizing is a personal choice, and sometimes it's more than is necessary. It does, however, make it much easier to locate a spice you need when you're in a hurry. Once you do the alphabetizing, it's done. Then when you need a spice, you'll be able to find it quickly; and in order to maintain your system, all you'll need to do is put the spice back in the empty space where it came from.

8. Discard old tea. Tazo Tea recommends that a shelf life for its tea—unopened and stored in a cool, dry place—is up to one year. Drinking a cup of tea made from a tea bag that's older than a year won't hurt you; however, the tea may take on other flavors or become weak.

9. Keep tea bags organized. One of my favorite kitchen organizing products is a tea organizer with individual compartments for teabags. You may have seen something similar at restaurants; when you ask for tea, the waiter brings you a box with many selections inside. I use an acrylic version with six compartments as well as a wicker one with twelve. They're nice enough to leave on the counter and impress your friends when they come over. As for the extra teabags that won't fit in the tea organizer, you can stash them in their boxes on a top shelf, and then replenish the tea organizer as needed.

10. Use a seasoning packet holder. These are containers designed to hold packets such as sauce mixes, salad dressing mixes, drink mixes, and taco seasonings. They come in a variety of textures, styles, and shapes and are excellent for keeping these packets together on a shelf. You can pull the entire container down and quickly locate what you're looking for. You may find that you need more than one to organize packets by category, since each one typically has only two or three sections. In Cynthia and Ron's kitchen we placed the spice pack holder on the top shelf along with the canned goods and turntables (photo 10). Again, like the plastic bin that holds baking supplies, the spice pack holder can easily be grabbed to see its entire contents.

11. Store baking supplies together. Gather up all of the following: baking soda, baking powder, vanilla, other flavorings, food coloring, sprinkles for cookies, frosting, cupcake tins, and maybe even candles for a cake. Find a container that fits the depth of one of your cupboards and is big enough to store the number of items you use on a regular basis. This will keep them all together, so when it's time to whip up a batch of cookies or cupcakes, you'll have everything you need at your fingertips.

12. Use plastic containers. These work great for items you use frequently that come in plastic bags, such as beans, rice, pasta, and nuts. Using containers eliminates the possibility of the contents spilling out and makes them look much neater on your shelf. It also helps to keep out unwanted guests such as bugs.

13. Store canned goods on can risers. Can risers are like bleachers for your canned goods. They allow you to see canned goods placed behind one another because each row is on a different level (photo 10). There are several kinds on the market, but they all serve the same purpose. Most have three levels, and some are even expandable to fit your space. If you set cans on the shelf in front of the can riser, you'll end up with four levels to use. I try to use can risers in cupboards with shelves that aren't so deep that the product and the cans get swallowed up. You can also use can risers in a pantry, but typically the shelves are deeper, so there ends up being a lot of wasted space.

14. Keep grocery bags corralled. If you're like me and keep the plastic bags that your groceries come in, then you can't live without a grocery bag organizer. Simple Human makes my favorite version of this product. In fact, I love it so much that I have four of them in my home. They're under the kitchen sink, in the laundry room next to the litter box, in the master bathroom under the sink, and in the upstairs bathroom under the sink.

Simple Human's organizer has heavy-duty sticky tape that holds it securely to the door. Or, if you prefer, you can use the screws that come with it to install the organizer on the inside of the door or on the wall. There are many other versions of this product available, in both plastic and canvas.

15. Label your containers. Labeling is another organizing practice that is a personal choice. For some, labeling is a necessity in order to remember where something belongs, or what's in a container. Others don't need to label for themselves, but do so to make sure that other family members know where things belong. If you use plastic or glass containers for items that you use on a regular basis, such as rice, beans, and walnuts, consider labeling the containers with the contents. If you store them on a pull-out shelf, consider labeling the lid instead, since you'll see that rather than the front of the containers.

16. Store little-used entertaining items out of the way. If you have items that you use only occasionally, when entertaining, put them in hard-to-reach locations. A great place is above the refrigerator or on the top shelves of cabinets. You may also want to consider storing them close to but not in the kitchen, such as in a utility room or a cabinet in the garage.

Cynthia had a lot of vases that were scattered throughout the kitchen. We chose to put them above the refrigerator. We placed several small vases in two separate plastic bins that could be easily removed from the cupboard when she is looking for the perfect vase or vases for entertaining.

17. Keep all lunch supplies in one place, in order to eliminate the morning chaos while getting the kids off to school. Lunch bags, sandwich bags, twist ties, napkins, plastic silverware, and spare change may all fall into this category. Food-related items for lunches, such as drink boxes, protein bars, raisins, and chips, can also be kept together in a bin inside a cupboard or pantry, so you can pull out the bin and have everything at your fingertips when you're packing lunches.

18. Be aware of product expiration dates.

19. Ensure that all family members know where things go. Cynthia told me that she was afraid to have her daughters unload the dishwasher lest they put some things where they didn't belong. After you've spent your valuable time organizing, the last thing you want is for someone in the family to mess up your new system by not putting things in the proper place. Avoid this headache and use sticky notes on the outsides of your cabinets and drawers to label the contents. You can remove them in a few days or weeks depending on how long it takes for your family to adjust to your newly organized kitchen.

CHAPTER **5**

CLOSET

Think for a moment how great it would be if you could open the doors of your closet each morning and have a well-organized space where you could see everything you own and you could pull together an outfit in two seconds. A dream, you might be thinking. No, this is reality, and you can achieve it! By the time you're finished reading and working through this chapter, you'll be inspired to declutter your closet and start reaping the rewards.

Let's explore a few reasons why your closet may be in need of a little clutter cleanup. "But I might wear it someday." Does that ever-popular phrase sound familiar? How about this one: "I have nothing to wear." This is often said by people whose closets are stuffed with clothes. The reason most of my clients claim they have nothing to wear, I've found, is that they can't see what they own, so they can't pull an outfit together.

Although there are many different kinds of closets in the home, this chapter focuses on the master clothes closet. The organizing principles presented here will apply equally well to all of the other closets in your home, including the closets of other family members.

A local journalist wrote an article on closet organizing and simple ideas for getting ready in the morning. She asked me for tips and product ideas, and at the end of her article she mentioned that I was looking for a closet to feature in this book. You can imagine how many inquiries I received! The photos ranged all the way from fairly organized closets to closets that weren't being used at all because their owners couldn't find anything in them.

I selected the messiest closet submitted, that of Ashley Williams, to organize and make over. Today you would not even recognize Ashley's closet—the transformation was unbelievably quick and absolutely amazing!

ASHLEY'S STORY

When I spoke to Ashley on the phone, she told me that her home was nice but she felt she had trashed one area. She was living out of laundry bins in her bedroom because she couldn't use her master closet. She had been living in her home for almost six years and had never been able to use the closet; it had quickly become a dumping ground for anything that didn't have a "home," and the door was shut to keep it all in. As far as she was concerned, it was a forbidden zone.

Ashley said she spent thousands of dollars every year replacing clothes and other items because she couldn't find anything—it was all buried in the closet. She couldn't even find a matching pair of shoes to wear. "I feel guilty that I have a lot of nice things and a nice house," Ashley said, "but I'm not taking care of what I have."

Ashley said she had tried in the past to organize her closet, but it was just too overwhelming. Her mom, who is very organized, had volunteered to help on several occasions, but Ashley thought this was something she needed to do on her own. She also felt that if she had to pay for the closet to be organized, she would be even more motivated to keep it organized afterward. Ultimately, Ashley was excited about the prospect of getting her closet organized once

PROJECT BREAKDOWN — TOTAL HOURS (29)

TASK	HOURS
Sorting, purging, and organizing	23
Ashley's shopping and installation time	2
Laura's shopping and installation time	2
Hauling away to garage sale	1
Cleanup	1
Total project time	**29 HOURS**

and for all, and showing her family and boyfriend that she too could have an organized closet.

I selected Ashley for two reasons. First of all, I loved Ashley's personality and willingness to change her ways. The willingness to change and live a more organized life is truly the first step toward being organized. Secondly, I knew it would be a difficult project to tackle, not just because of the amount of stuff but also because of the closet's unusual layout. I felt that if we organized a very challenging closet, containing an overwhelming amount of stuff, this would illustrate that you could certainly organize your own closet based on our techniques.

THE PROCESS

1. Dedicate time.

As with all organizing projects, you'll need to dedicate time to tackle your closet or closets. In Ashley's case, she had Presidents' Day off from work, so we dedicated a good part of that day to organizing her closet. If you have an entire day to dedicate, you'll see huge changes at the end of the day, as we did. If you don't have an entire day, don't let that delay you from getting started; you can do a little bit each day. Just keep in mind that it will take you a bit longer to see the dramatic results. Even if you have only 10 or 15 minutes a day to work on your closet, use this time wisely and work on sorting through a few inches of your closet at a time—or sort through one box at a time.

2. Gather supplies.

When organizing your closet, you won't need too many supplies, just a few empty boxes or bags for donations and maybe a trash can. A rolling garment rack would be very useful too, but it's not a necessity.

For Ashley's closet, we used garbage bags to hold the clothes and shoes she didn't want, and we used several bags for garbage.

3. Establish a staging area.

Because of the amount of stuff in Ashley's closet, I knew we would need several staging areas where we could place things as they were being removed from the closet. A staging area can be any location outside the area that you're organizing. You'll use it during steps 4–6.

Space was pretty tight in Ashley's bedroom because there were four of us working on her closet, including Ashley. We decided to use her bathroom (which was next to the closet), her bed, and the floor around the bed, as well as the hallway outside her bedroom, as our staging areas. In the hallway, we placed our garment rack to hang clothes as we removed them from the closet. We used the bathroom to sort anything that wasn't clothing related (photo 4), and we used her bed and the floor around her bed for all clothing-related items (photo 3).

You'll want to choose a staging area that gives you plenty of space to pull items out of your closet as you are organizing. You may even wish to use another room as part of your staging area.

4. Sort.

Let the sorting begin! Ashley had a lot of stuff that needed to be sorted, and not all of it was clothing. In fact, there was so much stuff, even on the floor, that in some parts of the closet it was about three feet high (photo 1). Because there was no possible way that we could all fit in the closet, I assigned different people from our team to specific parts of the sorting phase. Nancy was responsible for all non-clothing items, Dori was responsible for all clothing and shoes, and Ashley was responsible for making decisions as fast as possible!

Sometimes the most challenging aspect of organizing is knowing where to begin. In this case, we needed to start at the

THREE COMMON PROBLEMS OF CLOSETS

1. You can't find anything to wear!

2. There's not enough space for the current contents.

3. You have no idea how to maximize the space in the closet.

①

②

① One of the first pictures taken of Ashley's closet when I arrived. The view is from the back of the closet looking out to the hall. We had to stand on top of the three-foot pile of stuff on the floor of the closet in order to take the picture.

② These shelves had linens and clothes tossed on them in no particular organized fashion.

③ At the beginning of our sort, we used Ashley's bed to sort clothing, shoes, and books into groups. As we needed more room to sort clothes, we moved books to the staging area in the bathroom and shoes into plastic bags.

③

❹ The bathroom, including the tub, was used as one of our staging areas for things such as luggage, office supplies, books, gifts, lotions, and bath products, plus a few items for the garage. These items would later be moved to the appropriate locations in Ashley's home.

❺ The top of Ashley's toilet (with the lid closed and draped with a towel) had linens stacked on top. Her counter top was used to hold gift wrap and ribbons.

❻ All of Ashley's flip-flops were temporarily stored in a plastic garbage bag in order to corral them all together as we sorted through her shoes. Later, her flip-flops were organized into hanging shoe storage.

❻

❼

❽

❿

❼ All of the wire hangers that we removed from Ashley's closet that were no longer being used. They were a jumbled, tangled mess in her closet, just taking up valuable space that could be better served for hanging clothes.

❽ This under-the-bed storage container that had been tossed in the middle of Ashley's closet is now being used to store Ashley's memorabilia, such as old T-shirts and shoes that had special meaning to her. The container was later placed under her bed.

❾ Bins on shelves were used to contain items such as scarves, purses, and wallets.

10 This hanging shoe organizer was used to store Ashley's flip-flops, tennis shoes, and other casual shoes that she didn't wear every day.

11 The front walkway and part of Ashley's front yard were used to stage all of the garbage, donations, and items that would be sold in the garage sale, including white stacking organizing bins that no longer served a purpose.

front of the closet on the floor and work our way in. I started pulling out the first things on the floor in the front of the closet and divided them into clothing and non-clothing items. Non-clothing went on my left side, to be scooped up and sorted by Nancy in the bathroom, and clothing items were set on my right side and pulled into the bedroom by Dori.

Nancy and Dori were each responsible for further sorting these items into categories, so that Ashley could quickly look at the various groups of things she had stored in the closet and make decisions about them. Here are some of the categories of items we came up with:

Clothing

Shoes: casual, dressy, flip-flops (photo 6)

Clothes: sweaters, coats, skirts, dresses, jeans, casual pants, pajamas, socks, underwear, bras, swimsuits, scarves, bathing suit wraps, shirts, blouses, T-shirts, bathrobes, belts, boyfriend's clothes

Non-clothing

Linens: blankets, sheets, towels, pillowcases, pillows, beach towels

Luggage: suitcases, duffel bags, purses, wallets

Home decor: baskets, picture frames, dried flowers, photos, photo albums

Office supplies: pens, pencils, paper, notebooks, measuring tape, staples, paper clips

Gifts: a wide assortment of gifts that had been purchased but never given

Bathroom products: lotions, makeup, bubble bath, cotton, shaving lotion

Miscellaneous: old shopping bags, receipts, stuffed animals, camera

The best find of the day came about four hours into the project, when we found a 35mm camera that Ashley had spent two years looking for! Ashley had asked us earlier in the day if we had found the camera, and we had not yet run across it at that point, so we were thrilled to find it as the day progressed.

The sorting process took us about 16 hours total (four hours per person). Remember, there were four of us working on this project, so the hours added up quickly!

5. Purge.

While we were doing the sorting, Ashley had already begun some of the purging. When we arrived at Ashley's home, she told us that about 80 percent of the clothes in the closet could probably be tossed or donated because she had not worn them for several years. I could tell that Ashley was more than ready to have an organized closet if she was already talking about letting go of so much before we had even gotten started. "Way to go, Ashley!" I told her.

Let's talk about letting go. Forget about the phrase "But I might wear it someday." Typically, you'll wear only about 20 percent of what's in your closet on a regular basis. Why? Because we all have a tendency to gravitate toward the clothes that we love, that make us look great, and that we feel good in. After all, who wants to wear something that doesn't make them look or feel good?

I remember the days when I used to shop just to buy clothes. The eye-opening moment for me was the day I hired an image consultant, Audrey Beaulac, to help me create a personal style for myself. After Audrey did an initial assessment, we took a trip into my closet. Even though it was organized, what I found fascinating was the number of clothes that Audrey pulled out of my closet that weren't my style.

Audrey and I hauled the clothing she'd pulled out into one of my spare bedrooms (my staging area), and she told me I needed to let them go. Of course I had to remind myself what I tell people every day—I wasn't going to miss them, and the amount of money that I'd spent on the clothes no longer mattered to me. And I was exactly right. The next day I took all of the clothing to a local women's shelter. I felt great about donating the clothes, and I've never missed even one item. In fact, I can't even remember what I donated anymore.

What this experience taught me was that even though my closet was organized, I was hanging on to more clothes than I needed. The truth of the matter
was that I wasn't wearing them anyway, because they didn't make me look good
and I didn't feel good wearing them. I can now say that I know what it's like to
have someone come into your closet and help you purge—because I've been on
that side of the equation too.

Today, I leave a box in my closet for clothing that is to be donated or taken
to a consignment store. If I put something on and it no longer looks good or
makes me feel great, it goes in the box. When the box is full, it goes into the
car and gets dropped off.

Ashley did a fantastic job of letting go. In fact, she ended up letting go of 19
large garbage bags full of clothes that she had not been wearing (photo 11). I
believe at least one of those bags was entirely full of shoes. The garbage bags
we used were 33-gallon bags, so you can imagine the amount of clothing that
was eliminated! As for the non-clothing items, Ashley let go of about half of
them.

We also discarded a couple of different organizing products that were no
longer working for Ashley. It's important to keep in mind that if the product
no longer works for the items you're trying to store, it may be time to look for
something different. Specifically, we discarded several under-bed storage boxes
that weren't being used under the bed but had stuff tossed in them instead. We
also eliminated a three-level plastic stacking shoe rack (photo 11) as well as
a rolling wire unit with three shelves that had became a catchall for anything
Ashley didn't know what to do with.

6. Group like items together.

As you probably noticed during this project, we started grouping like items
together during the sorting phase. This made it easy for Ashley to see everything in a particular category and to make an informed decision—because she
was able to see the quantities of everything. For example, we grouped the following items together in certain areas:

Bathroom: linens, gift wrap, luggage, body lotions and bubble bath, books, home decor items, office supplies, gifts (photos 4 and 5)

Bed: scarves, shoes, shirts, dresses, jeans, belts (photo 3)

Under-bed storage box: memorabilia, such as old T-shirts and shoes that Ashley wanted to keep, but that didn't need to be kept in her closet any longer (photo 8)

When you're working on your closet, you may want to group items together into categories as you sort though things, as we did. This will help you save time along the way, by not having to re-sort.

7. Examine your space.

Once the area you're organizing is just about empty, you can begin to assess your space. You'll want to think about how you're going to use the newly transformed area. Ask yourself: What purpose does this closet now serve? What types of items are now going to call the closet home? These questions will help you determine how to maximize the space in your closet.

Ashley's closet had wire shelving that had previously been installed. We knew when we started the project that installing a new closet system wasn't an option. I would have loved to have worked with one of our closet vendors to install a custom-built system in Ashley's closet, but in reality, this is not an option that's possible for everyone. Instead, what I wanted to feature in this closet was how you can transform your existing closet by clearing out the clutter and using the space differently.

Here are some specific closet organizing products that can help you maximize the use of your space:

- Baskets of all shapes, sizes, and textures.

- Hanging belt and tie organizers. Use these for hanging purses as well!

- Hanging shoe and sweater bags. Use these for more than shoes and sweaters—they make great organizers for scarves, mittens and gloves, underwear, socks, and even purses. Some hanging shoe and sweater bags also come with pull-out drawers that fit on the shelves (photo 10).

▶ Shelf dividers. These keep sweaters, workout clothes, and jeans from falling on top of each other.

▶ Floor-based shoe organizers. There are so many options to choose from, it's best to determine how many shoes you have first!

▶ Hanging clear vinyl handbag organizers.

▶ See-through garment bags—excellent to store cocktail or formal attire that you want to be able to see at a glance.

▶ Over-the-door hooks. These are excellent for holding and organizing your bathrobe, a work outfit, a pair of pajamas, or any clothing that you may wear frequently and want quick access to.

8. Shop!

From the "before" photos of Ashley's closet (photos 1 and 2), you might have thought she would need a lot of products to create more space. In reality, because Ashley got rid of so much, we didn't need many products to help her control the chaos! We used some very simple products that are listed on page 69. You'll also notice the purpose that each of these products serve.

9. Install products.

Installing products in your closet can be either quick and simple or time consuming and complex. In Ashley's closet, installation took about an hour and consisted of the following:

Shoe organizers: We used three kinds—a combination of floor-based and hanging. Which shoes would be placed where was determined by frequency of use. The floor-based unit, placed closest to the front of the closet, was used to store the shoes that Ashley wears daily (see the photo at the beginning of the chapter). The hanging shoe bag that holds 10 pairs of shoes was used to organize her dress shoes, and the hanging storage unit that held 20 pairs was used to store the rest (photo 10).

Chrome-plated four-prong hanger: We hung all her belts on this handy organizer.

Wire shelf divider: We placed this between the two stacks of jeans that sit on top of her shelf.

Plastic bins: We placed these on the floor and sorted purses and scarves into the bins until we could determine the correct-size bin to store each of these items in (photo 9).

PRODUCT LIST

STORE	ITEM/SERVICE	SIZE	COST	TOTAL $
Lillian Vernon	Rattan shoe chest			139.98
	Chrome-plated four-prong hangers		set of 2	9.98
	Garment covers	extra large	set of 6	7.98
			total	157.94
Other Stores	Hanging shoe bag	holds 10 pairs		19.95
	Hanging shoe bag	holds 20 pairs		34.95
	Wire shelf dividers			3.95
	Plastic bins in various sizes		several	14.50
	White plastic hangers			10.00
			total	83.35
			TOTAL COST OF CLOSET PRODUCTS	**$241.29**

Garment covers: As a finishing touch, we placed garment covers over the tops of some of Ashley's dress clothes to protect them from dust.

10. Maintain.

Now that the closet is organized, there's just one final, ongoing step: maintenance. This may seem like a challenge if you're not used to keeping your closet orderly every day. But it's really quite easy and won't take you much time. It's just a matter of hanging your clothes back in their appropriate places and putting your shoes back in the place you designated for them. Sound simple? It is, but you'll need to do it every day.

You'll also want to resist the urge to store things in the closet that are not meant to have a permanent home there. Once you begin to use your closet to store things that don't belong there, it may once again become a dumping ground for anything that doesn't have a place.

Ashley's master closet was the one area in her home where she would toss stuff that didn't have a place. It became easy to shut the door on it, but that meant she couldn't use her closet or find any clothes to wear, which was why she was living out of her laundry baskets.

When we had completed most of her closet, we suspended our work for about three weeks while I waited for a few last products to be shipped. I was concerned that when I came back to Ashley's closet, it might not look as I had left it—that she might slip back into her old habits. But I was pleasantly surprised! When I returned to apply the finishing touches, Ashley's closet was immaculate. She had done an excellent job of maintaining the new system we had created. Ashley truly had been inspired to keep her closet organized, and she even indicated that it was quite simple to maintain.

When we finished Ashley's closet, she told me that she no longer felt stressed out. When she looks in her closet now, she feels calm and can find exactly what she is looking for—without running all over the house for a matching shoe or a particular shirt she wanted to wear.

I hope you were inspired by Ashley's story. If you need more motivation, here's an interesting fact: Real estate professionals regard "first impression" improvements such as decluttering the closets to be one of the smartest ways to prepare a home for sale. Yes—by lightening the load, your closet will appear larger than it is. A potential buyer of your home wants to be able to visualize their clothes in your closet—not look at the disorganized contents of your closet.

CLOSET ORGANIZING TIPS

Although each closet in your home will contain different types of items, you can still use the process above to sort, purge, and group similar items together and then reassess and repurpose your space. Here are some tips to help you declutter your closets:

1. **Go through your closet and pull out all of the empty hangers.** You might be surprised by how much space they're taking up. Sort them by type—for example, put all of the shirt hangers together and all of the pant hangers together. Chances are you don't need all of them; assess how many you have of each type, and then toss or donate the ones you no longer need.

2. **Eliminate all the wire hangers.** Check with your dry cleaner to see if they recycle them (photo 7). Toss used plastic bags from dry cleaning.

3. **Establish a location in your closet to hang the remaining empty hangers.** This makes it simple to find a hanger when you need it and will keep hangers from getting tangled in with clothing already on hangers.

4. **Place a small over-the-door rack on the back of the closet door or bathroom door.** It's an excellent way to hold and organize your bathrobe, a pair of pajamas, or any clothing you wear frequently and want quick access to. It's also a great temporary place to hang the outfit you plan to wear that day. Leave the hangers on the rack. When you return from

work, you can return the clothes to the hangers (the ones that don't need to be laundered) and place them back in the closet.

5. Purchase a hanging belt organizer—a hanger specifically designed to hold belts. They typically have two sides that you can slide the belt buckles on.

6. If you don't have drawers or shelves in your closet, consider using plastic bins, baskets, or wooden shirt boxes to store items such as shirts, sweaters, jeans and pants, workout clothes, pajamas, purses, and scarves. This will give your shelves a clean, uncluttered look as well as help to hold everything in its place. You'll notice on page 63 that in Ashley's closet we used three plastic bins to hold all of her purses and two bins to hold her scarves. We kept the lids (not pictured) on the scarf boxes so we could stack them and also keep Ashley's cats from turning the bins into their beds. We left the lids off the purse bins so that Ashley could easily grab the purse she needed. The extra lids were stacked in the corner of her closet—out of the way but accessible, in case she needs to use them in the future.

7. Two common ways of organizing the hanging clothes in a closet are by color and by type of clothing. If you choose to organize your clothes by type, you might want to consider grouping the following together: sleeveless shirts, T-shirts, short-sleeve blouses or shirts, long-sleeve blouses or shirts, sweaters, jackets, jeans, skirts, suits, dresses, formal/cocktail attire, scarves, belts, and workout clothes.

Within each of these categories, if you want to take your organization one step further, you could organize the clothes from light to dark, or divide them even further by grouping solid colors from light to dark and then your patterned clothing from light to dark within each type of clothing.

8. Having difficulty remembering when you last wore a piece of clothing? Try hanging all of your clothes facing in the opposite direction. When you wear them, hang them back on the rack facing the way you would normally hang them. After six months or a year, look at the hangers that are still facing in the opposite direction; this will tell you which clothes you haven't worn, and you can then decide whether you want them to continue taking up space in your closet.

9. Double-hanging clothes will provide you with lots of additional space in your closet. If your current closet is configured with just one rod or wire shelf, consider using a hanging rod that will give you an additional level for clothes. Or you could remove the existing rod or shelf and install two, thus giving you twice the amount of storage space.

10. When determining how much hanging space you need, assess how many inches of clothing you have that will be "short-hung," such as shirts, versus clothing that will be "long-hung," such as pants, skirts, and dresses. When calculating your space, decide whether you want your pants to be hung long or folded over a hanger. Knowing how you want to store your pants will make a big difference when laying out your closet.

11. As a nice finishing touch to your closet, use just one type or color of hanger. This will provide you with a consistent look and feel. In Ashley's closet we used white plastic hangers (photo 9) for most of her clothes and oversized blue plastic hangers for her sweaters. This was Ashley's choice. Personally, I love wooden hangers. They're beautiful and look very classy in any type of closet.

M ost likely, your master closet is something you use on a daily basis. By organizing it and keeping it orderly, you'll reap so many rewards. It will be much easier to find clothing and put together an outfit when you can see what you have. It will also make shopping much easier and more productive, because you'll know what clothing you need to purchase to help fill in any gaps you have in your wardrobe. I hope you've been inspired to organize your closet or closets, and that you'll soon be enjoying the fruits of your labor!

Home offices often serve more than one purpose. They may be a place to pay bills, send personal e-mails, make sales, conduct conferences calls, do homework—and everything in between. And that may explain why many home offices look like a tornado hit them. If this describes your space, read on to find out how you can create a solution that will calm the storm.

Some of the personal stories in this book have a specific theme. The theme of this chapter's story is "maintenance." As you know from reading chapter 1, maintenance is step 10 in our process. It's a key element in any organizing project and needs to be practiced on a regular basis. Without regular maintenance, the system you create will break down, and you will have wasted your valuable time on this process.

When I invited people to submit their projects for possible inclusion in this book, I received the most entries in the home office category. Clearly, there was a lot of office chaos needing to be eliminated! To Sarah's credit, hers wasn't the worst office submitted; believe it or not, it was actually one of the better ones. With that said, you can still see by looking at our "before" photos (1, 2, and 3) that her office was far from organized.

Why did I select Sarah's office when it wasn't the worst project submitted? The main reason was that I really want you, the reader, to understand the importance of regular maintenance, whether in your own home office or throughout the rest of your home.

SARAH'S STORY

Sarah first became our client about two and a half years ago, when she called for help with her home office. It was then serving three purposes: as an office for her home-based business, as her personal office for day-to-day tasks such as bill paying and e-mail, and as a place for her daughter, Emily, to do her schoolwork. After five sessions, our work together was completed and it was up to Sarah to maintain her newly organized office.

When I put out a call for projects to feature in this book, Sarah contacted me to say that we needed to "organize my office—again." Typically, when I work with a client on an organizing project, my goal is to work myself out of a job. Once a client's new organizing system is established, I make sure they know where everything is and where it should be put when they're done with it. For those reasons, I was surprised that Sarah would be contacting me again.

THE PROCESS

I. Dedicate time.

To kick off the reorganizing of Sarah's office, we initially set aside one full day with me; Nancy, one of our consultants; and Sarah. Emily, Sarah's daughter, joined us after school. We also had to schedule two follow-up sessions as well as shopping. Although we had organized this office two and a half years earlier, we still ended up spending a total of 47 hours doing it again. Keep in mind that all organizing projects take time—which is one more reason to maintain the system you're going to create for yourself in your home office.

The wonderful thing about organizing an office is that offices have so many different components, you can easily divide the project into smaller pieces and organize one section at a time. For example, you may want to divide your office into the following bite-size pieces (OK, so some of them may seem like more

PROJECT BREAKDOWN	TOTAL HOURS 47
TASK	**HOURS**
Sorting, purging, and organizing	39
Sarah and Laura's shopping time	1
Sarah's shopping time	4
Installation time	1
Hauling away donations	1
Cleanup	1
Total project time	**47 HOURS**

of a mouthful): books, bills, computer cords and accessories, papers (active, nonactive, taxes, vital records, memorabilia), software, supplies, and non-office-related items that need to be removed from the office.

Don't feel as if you need to tackle your entire office in one clean sweep—you may end up feeling overwhelmed. Instead, after you've set aside the time to work on your office, make a list of the areas that need to be organized and set aside time for each. Resist the urge to put too much time in between each area that you'll be organizing. It's important to keep the ball rolling so that you'll see big changes in a short amount of time.

Remember the good news: It may have taken you years to get your office into its current state, but it won't take that long to organize it!

2. Gather supplies.

Gathering supplies for organizing your office is as simple as a quick trip through your home to gather a few of the basics. You will not need to make a special trip to the store to get supplies—remember, shopping is step 8 and it will be so much more enjoyable and productive once you know what you need.

Here are a few of the basics you will need:

➡ Empty boxes for the following categories: donations, recycling, shredding, and items that belong in other rooms

➡ Garbage can, or garbage bags

➡ Sticky notes for labeling

➡ A pen or marker

➡ File folders if you're going to be organizing papers

3. Establish a staging area.

Because it's close to impossible to complete the next three steps of the project without having an adequate space to work in, you'll want to create a staging area where you can place things as you begin to sort through them.

Sarah had a very large office with an open feel to it. Although she had a lot of floor space to use for sorting, we still decided to use her hallway as our staging area. We moved things to the hall that needed to be out of the way: extra chairs, an old computer to be donated, and items that were no longer going to be kept in Sarah's office. We also set our box for donations in this area, and each time we came across something to be donated, it was immediately put into the box, so that no more time needed to be spent looking at that item or making another decision about it.

The important thing to keep in mind when choosing a staging area is that you want one with enough space so that you're not tripping over things as you work, and so that you can see the different categories of items that you're holding on to.

With our staging area established and our supplies on hand, we were ready to start sorting through the mounds of papers on Sarah's desk and all of the books on her long bookshelves.

4. Sort.

In Sarah's office we began our sorting in two areas at the same time. Nancy tackled the bookshelves, and I worked on everything on the desk, under the desk, and in the cabinets above the desk.

At the beginning of the project, we established that only books and photos would be kept on the bookshelves, and nothing would be kept on the top of the bookshelves anymore. Things placed on top of the bookshelves could be seen from the living room below when piled too high. Take a look at "before" photo 3 of the bookshelves and how cluttered they look, with books lying every which way and some just stuffed wherever space could be found. Bookshelves can look attractive, even if they're holding a lot of books, as you'll see later on in the chapter.

In an initial pass through the bookshelves and the top of the bookshelves, we discovered the following types of misplaced items, which were all removed and placed in groups on the floor for Sarah to look at. All of these items would

1. You have no usable filing system.

2. You keep too many papers, newspapers, and magazines because there's no system to process the information that you want to retain.

3. You have more books than will fit on the existing bookshelves.

4. The electronic cords and cables under your desk are a tangled and twisted mess.

5. You can't find the computer software when the computer technician needs it.

6. Late fees are assessed on bills because you can't find
→

ultimately need to find a new home in the office: music CDs, software CDs, game CDs, reference CDs, empty boxes from cell phones and software, miscellaneous notebooks, artwork, and various electronic cords.

Look closely at photo 5 of the CDs stacked in different piles. Nancy not only gathered all of the CDs together but also divided them by category, into either music, software, games, or reference CDs—each of which would later need its own place to be stored.

Secondly, Nancy removed the books one by one and placed them in stacks on the floor, on the shelves, and on the top of the shelves in order to sort them into categories. You can see from photo 4 of the books on the shelves with the sticky notes how Nancy has begun to separate them into the categories below. Sarah had so many books that she had trouble locating a specific one quickly when she needed it, especially for her work as a lactation consultant. The categories of books that Nancy came up with for Sarah are as follows: home and garden, art, music, drama, religion, fiction and nonfiction, pets, coffee-table books, language books, travel and maps, self-help, health, reference, medical (birthing and lactation), and Emily's school yearbooks.

If you have books stored in your home office, consider creating a similar list of categories. If you're unsure of what categories your books fall into, you can start by pulling books out and seeing what goes together. You might even determine that a particular category of book doesn't need to be kept in your office, and that those books can be placed in another area of your home.

While all of Nancy's sorting was taking place, Sarah and I had a lot of sorting to do ourselves. We started with the desk surface, which was littered with papers, CDs, office supplies, and notebooks, as you can see in photo 1. On one corner of the desk was Emily's schoolwork, notebooks, textbooks, school supplies, and many items that belonged in either her bedroom or her bathroom. I began with the desk surface because we needed space to work on, and Sarah had a lot of it to use, if only we could find it!

I quickly scooped up a handful of papers and did a quick sort. Most of what I found was trash, such as fax cover sheets, scraps of paper with notes written on them, expired insurance policies, bills that had been paid, and so on. I made two piles for Sarah to look at: one pile of papers that I thought were trash, and another pile of papers that we needed to keep and establish a place for. I handed Sarah one stack of papers at a time and told her whether I thought it was trash or papers to keep.

I felt it was important for Sarah to take a quick look at the trash, to ensure that none of the scraps of paper had an important piece of information on it. About 99 percent of the trash I handed Sarah did indeed turn out to be tossable, and it then went immediately into the recycling or shredding box. Sarah didn't have any problem letting go of the paper once I told her it was stuff she didn't need; in fact, she sorted it right over the top of the recycling and shredding boxes.

The second stack of papers was much smaller, consisting of documents I felt she either needed or might want to keep as memorabilia. (See, I really don't make people get rid of everything!) Again, Sarah sorted this pile of papers over the recycling and shredding boxes. Much to my surprise, she probably let go of about a third of that stack of papers as well. This left us with a very small amount of paper that we needed to deal with later.

them and get them paid on time.

7. You can't quickly retrieve important documents and information, such as insurance policies, passports, transcripts, or passwords, because there's no established location for them.

8. You have an excessive amount of office supplies because you're never sure what you already have or because, like many of our clients, you just love to buy office supplies!

9. You don't file your taxes on time because you've lost the supporting documentation.

10. You lose important information due to a computer virus or failure, because you don't have a backup system in place.

①

③

① Sarah's office before our organizing makeover, with piles of paper and books littering the work surface—as well as equipment not being used. On the right side of the photo were all of Emily's books and supplies, as well as items that didn't need to be stored in the office area.

2

4

2 Piles of paper were scattered across the top of Sarah's desk. Most were papers that could have either been recycled or shred immediately. Some could have been filed immediately or placed in a "to be filed" basket.

3 Books, binders, office supplies, software, CDs, and more litter the bookshelves. The bookshelves were so full of items lying every which way that it was difficult to find a book.

4 Books divided into categories that would be purged and then placed on shelves in sections for each category: home and garden, art, music, drama, religion, fiction and nonfiction, pets, coffee-table, language, travel and maps, self-help, health, reference, medical (birthing and lactation), and Emily's school yearbooks.

5

6

5 CDs divided into categories of software, music, reference, and games. This allowed Sarah to sort through the CDs quickly to see which needed to be kept and which belonged in the office.

9

6 The supplies were pulled from several different areas throughout the office and sorted into groups of like items on the floor. Our categories consisted of office supplies, cables and computer accessories, empty cardboard boxes, phone books, nursing supplies, software manuals, and directories.

7

8

7 Cords ran in every direction under Sarah's work surface and were a terrible eyesore.

8 Using cord bundlers from 3M, cords were rolled up, bound together, and attached to the wall, keeping the cords off the floor—they're no longer eyesores.

9 With the cabinet reorganized, we were still able to use the magazine holders to divide the supplies and other items into sections that could be easily pulled out. Our breakdown consisted of software manuals, directories, loose-leaf paper, spiral notebooks and specialty papers, folders, and notebooks. The top shelf now contained all oversize envelopes.

10 Decorative red storage boxes were used to store photos of each family member. The boxes look pretty on the shelf and make a great place to place photos until there is time to put them in an album or scrapbook.

10

Remember that I scooped up just a handful of papers to sort. I didn't gather and sort all of Sarah's papers on the desk at one time; rather, I did it in bits and pieces throughout the day. Paper seems to be the most overwhelming—not to mention time-consuming—item for people to go through and make decisions about, so I didn't want Sarah to have to focus on all of her papers at one time. Instead, I divided the paper-sorting task into what I considered to be bite-size, manageable pieces for her.

While Sarah was busy looking through the paper stacks I had given her, I started working on sorting the rest of the items on the desk, underneath the desk, and in the cabinets. I grouped them on the floor in the following categories, as can be seen in photo 6: office supplies (paper, envelopes, pens, file folders, notebooks, blank CDs, sticky notes), cables and computer accessories, empty cardboard boxes, phone books, nursing supplies, software manuals, and directories.

As you begin to sort through items in your office, keep in mind that you first need to establish what purpose you want the space to serve. As you're sorting, if you find items that don't serve that purpose, put them in the box you've designated for items that need to be moved to other locations. Don't worry about moving them to their new location immediately; remember, the key is to stay focused on the job at hand. Place them inside the box, and distribute them throughout your home later.

5. Purge.

As you read in the previous step, Sarah had already begun to purge a lot of paper during the sorting process, which is perfectly acceptable. However, there was a lot more purging to be done. Remember all of those books and other items Nancy sorted? Well, Sarah needed to take a look at those items as well to see what she truly wanted to keep. She knew she would never read a lot of her books again, so those could be donated. It was much easier and quicker for her to make those decisions after Nancy had sorted the books into categories.

We even found a few duplicate books that we may not have noticed had we not sorted the books into categories.

Sarah ended up letting go of a lot of books, which she later donated. They filled a very large moving box that was so heavy we couldn't move it out of the room ourselves. My photographer, Adam, and his assistant had to step in to move it down to the living room. Sarah also let go of a lot of old software that was now out of date as well as old computer accessories and cables that she was no longer using. Most of the other things Sarah eliminated were just trash, items that would have had no value to anyone else and so couldn't be donated.

Paper and books were the major components of the mess in Sarah's office. I believe we emptied our recycling box at least four times the first day.

Letting go of books can be extremely difficult for some people. I've worked with clients who felt they simply had to keep every book they had ever purchased, even though they didn't have the space to store them. If books are a challenge for you, I suggest that you look at the amount of space you have throughout your house and determine which areas books could be kept in, while keeping together books in the same genre or category.

If you don't have enough space, it might be time to reconsider how many books you're keeping and whether you'll ever read or reference them again. In some cases, books may be so out of date that they no longer serve a purpose. Keep in mind that if you ever do need the book again, you'll likely be able to check out a copy from your library. If you choose to purge some of your books, see if your area has a bookstore that will buy books from you or offer you store credit. Of course, they may not accept everything you bring them, so you may still need to dispose of some of your books in another way.

6. Group like items together.

During the sorting phase of our project, as you'll recall, we had already begun to group like items together. This saved us time later on. The grouping phase is necessary so that when we get to the next phase, in which we examine the space we have to store and organize items, we can ensure that there's enough space for all the items we have.

Take, for example, Sarah's books. She had wall-to-wall bookshelves, two shelves tall (photos 3 and 10). We could tell we'd have enough room for all of the books she had decided to keep, just by eyeballing them. Office supplies, on the other hand, were the one type of item that Sarah seemed to lack the necessary space to store and contain. They were spread throughout the office in many different locations, probably because there was no single designated area where they were kept. With the office supplies all grouped together, though, it was very easy for us to determine what we needed to find a place for and what type of products might help us organize and store these items.

7. Examine your space.

When we looked at Sarah's space, we determined that there was only one major change necessary. We needed to find a location to store all of the small office supplies that had been strewn all over the room. We established that one of the cabinets above the desk would be used for Sarah's nursing supplies, and the other two would be used to store office supplies, phone books, and software. Specifically, regarding office supplies, we determined that envelopes of all sizes, notebooks, folders, notepads, and directories would be stored in the cabinets, but we would need to obtain some products that would help us contain them there. We also determined that we needed some type of product to place under her desk to contain and organize all of the small office supplies—such as pens, pencils, sticky notes, paper clips, rubber bands, stamps, and address labels.

We wanted to make a few smaller changes too, of course. Once we eliminated the piles of paper from the desk, for instance, we established that we did need a space on her desk for bills to be paid as well as an in-box, which you can see in the "after" photo of Sarah's office at the beginning of the chapter.

One consideration when thinking about storage in your office is whether you like to have things behind closed doors, such as in a cabinet or closet, or out in the open, such as on shelves. If you like things out in the open, you can still purchase products to keep items together on your shelves, to help keep the space from looking cluttered. Several examples of products you can use to do just this are listed in "Office Organizing Tips" at the end of this chapter.

While you're looking at your space, be sure to take measurements, and take them with you when you shop. For example, in Sarah's office, I made the following list of items to look for, and the necessary measurements, when we went shopping:

- Something with drawers to go under her desk and hold office supplies. We knew we had to find something less than 24 inches high with several drawers for items such as pens, pencils, and markers; notecards and sticky notes; printer toner; computer cables; stamps and return address labels; checkbooks; Emily's trinkets; camera supplies; and coupons and gift cards (see photo at the beginning of the chapter).

- Something to hold Sarah's membership cards and reward cards. She didn't always carry them with her, but we needed something that would keep them together.

- Something to hold about 15 pieces of software for her computer.

- Two in-boxes that we could place on her desk surface (see photo at the beginning of the chapter).

- Three boxes, no deeper than 10½ inches, to be placed on her bookshelves to hold photos—one box per family member (photo 10).

- A container to put memorabilia in, so Sarah could transfer them later to another area of her house.

- Cable organizers to tame the cord chaos under Sarah's desk (photo 8).

8. Shop!

Sarah and I had a plan, and we were armed with our list and measurements. We found everything we needed at various organizing supply stores.

PRODUCT LIST

STORE	ITEM/SERVICE	SIZE	COST	TOTAL $
Various Organizing Stores	*Cord bundlers from 3M*			2.99
	Cord clips from 3M	small and medium		5.98
	Cargo boxes (red) for photos		3 × 16.95	50.85
	In-boxes (black wire so Sarah could see through them)		2 × 3.95	7.90
	Plastic travel boxes (for membership cards and gift cards)		2 × .99	1.98
	Bin for memorabilia			3.95
	Software CD plastic storage box			3.95
	Three-drawer plastic cabinets		4 × 14.99	59.96
	Paper shredder			29.99
			TOTAL COST OF OFFICE PRODUCTS	**$167.55**

9. Install products.

After completing our shopping, we had just one set of products we needed to install: cord bundlers and cord clips. All of the other products just needed to be set in place (and, in the case of the drawers, labeled).

Cord bundlers and cord clips from 3M: We installed these products to help eliminate the cord chaos under Sarah's desk. Notice "before" photo 7 of the cords on the floor.

There were two issues with the cords. First, there were cords under the desk, such as extra DSL cables, that weren't being used and just needed to be eliminated. Second, we needed to move Sarah's computer as well as several items connected to it, such as the printer, monitor, keyboard, and mouse, so that she could sit comfortably at her desk. One of Sarah's big complaints about her office was how the computer had been set up. She continually hit her knees on the computer when she sat at her desk. Once we moved the necessary components, we needed to tame the cords using the cord bundlers and cord clips. I wrapped them in a circle and bound them with Velcro ties. I then attached them to the walls using the cord bundlers to keep them off the floor. The long cords for the DSL and the phone were attached to the wall using the cord clips, which held them high up on the wall, below the underside of the desk.

How do the cords under your desk look? They don't need to be a jumbled, tangled mess.

Boxes and baskets: We used our three red cargo boxes to hold current photos of each family member. The boxes were then placed at one end of a bookshelf, as you can see in "after" photo 10. The two black wire baskets you see on Sarah's desk were used for bills and items to be filed. Sarah wanted her bills in one of these baskets so that she could see what needed to be paid.

The last time we organized her office, there were systems she was unable to maintain. One was the bill-paying system. Previously, we had put all bills that needed to be paid in a "Bills to Pay" folder, which was then placed in a horizontal file holder on her desk. This didn't work well for Sarah, as it turned out, because she couldn't see the bills in the folder.

The lesson to be learned here is that if one system isn't working, and you've made an honest attempt for at least three weeks (which is about the amount of time it takes to form a new habit), then it may be time to tweak the system. In this case, we made a very minor adjustment, yet it made a major impact on her ability to pay bills in a timely fashion.

Plastic travel boxes for Sarah's membership cards and gift cards: The boxes we used were intended for soap, I believe, but they were the perfect size for the credit card–size cards. Using a label maker, we labeled each box so there would be no confusion.

Plastic bin for memorabilia: We filled this bin with the memorabilia we found in Sarah's office. It was then transferred to another area of her home until she was ready to deal with it. I know what you're thinking—I stored memorabilia in a plastic bin that's not acid-free? But it's actually OK: some of the items didn't need to be kept in acid-free storage, and Sarah assured me that the others would be transferred later to more permanent, appropriate storage. For more information on how to organize and store memorabilia, see chapter 12.

CD storage box: This was simple and quick. We put all of the software Sarah was keeping into the box, shut the lid, and placed the box in the cabinet above her desk.

Three-drawer plastic cabinets: These were filled with the items listed on page 89, labeled, and set into place. Both cabinets were close to the area of the desk that Sarah worked on daily and were now easy to access, and they helped to keep the clutter off her desk, so we accomplished two goals with these units.

Paper shredder: This was an important tool for the maintenance phase, which will be discussed in the next step.

Installing products in your home office may be as simple as this. Remember, organizing doesn't need to be complicated or expensive. By no means am I dismissing the idea of going out and purchasing new furniture for your office, such as a desk, bookshelves, or other storage units, if that's what you truly need. For Sarah's project, though, it wasn't necessary; she had all the storage necessary. We just needed to determine a better way for her to use and maintain the space.

10. Maintain.

We had finally reached the step where Sarah's organizing project had broken down two and a half years earlier: the maintenance phase. I believe the biggest challenge for Sarah was what to do with all of the paper. As you'll recall from the sorting phase, most of the paper we looked at was trash. In this case, the quick cure for the paper chaos was to immediately put paper that was no longer needed into the shredder or the recycling bin. One of the reasons paper had backed up in the past was Sarah's shredder didn't work. Now that she has a new one, she can shred paper trash immediately.

The papers Sarah kept were filed into the system we had established in our previous round of organizing. We added a couple of additional folders to her system because her needs had changed, but we still ended up with just one filing drawer each for personal and business papers.

The last bits of information that Sarah needed help storing were account numbers and passwords. Although this is a piece of her project that you can't see, it was a very important part of her new, organized office. Sarah uses Microsoft Outlook as her e-mail program, so we chose to use the "Contacts" section of Outlook to store this information. This way, when she synchronized her personal digital assistant (PDA) to her Outlook, she would have all of this information at her fingertips.

Many of these account numbers and passwords had simply been scribbled on scraps of paper on her desk, so they were difficult to locate, and she ran a big risk of losing very important information. Now they're all stored in one location, and she has a backup since the information is stored both on her PDA and on the computer.

For more information about how to organize using Microsoft Outlook, visit www.eliminatechaos.com, where you can purchase the book *Organizing and Customizing with Microsoft Outlook*.

OFFICE ORGANIZING TIPS

Clutter in your office, whether on your work surface or on the floor, can be extremely distracting. If you're used to working in this kind of environment, you may not even be aware that the clutter is distracting you. It also causes unnecessary stress, because the items lying around often represent unfinished business. Having a system and a place to put things in your office will help minimize the distractions and eliminate extra stress. Here are 10 tips to help you declutter your home office:

1. Bookshelves. When placing books on bookshelves, try grouping them by category. Instead of standing them all upright, try laying groups of books flat and stacked on top of each other. Bookshelves don't need to be full of books from one end to the other. In between the groups, you can display a photo or a special treasure to break up the sections a bit. Look at "after" photo 10 of our bookshelves to see how we organized Sarah's books.

2. Magazine holders. Magazine holders can serve many purposes besides just storing magazines. For instance, they can hold directories, software manuals, packages of computer labels, folders, dividers, packages of computer photo paper, warranties, or user guides (photo 9). When placing a magazine holder on a shelf, try turning it around so that you see the back of the holder instead of the contents. This way you end up with a very clean look. Label the holder if you can't remember what's in it.

3. Computer cords and cables. Label the cords and cables under your desk. Many products are available to do this; they can be found at your local office supply store or online. If you don't want to purchase something, use a piece of masking tape, make a flag around the cord, and label the tape. You can also attach a power strip to the underside of your desk so that the cords won't have to travel so far and don't bunch up on the floor. Notice in photo 8 how great the computer cords and cables look organized under Sarah's work surface.

4. Computer software. Eliminate your empty computer software boxes; you don't need them. What you do need is the product key, which will be located either on the box, on the CD case, or on the software itself. Store computer manuals in a magazine holder, and then store your software in either a box designed to hold the CDs in their cases, or in a binder. If you discard the cases the CDs came in, be sure to record the product key—without it, you won't be able to reinstall your software if that becomes necessary. You can use a label to record the name of the software as well as the product key on each of the slots in the binder. This way you'll know exactly where each piece of software should be kept. It will also save you from spending a lot of time looking for the correct CD when you're on the phone with computer support or when a computer technician is at your home. Keeping your software and manuals separate should not be a problem, since you don't often use both at the same time.

5. Stamps and return address labels. Establish one location in your office for these mailing supplies, including a return address stamp if you have one. Store them together, close to where you pay the bills, either in an envelope or in a specified compartment in a drawer.

6. Envelopes. If you use different sizes of envelopes, instead of going in and out of each box, use an envelope organizer to separate the different sizes. This is also a great place to store stamps and labels. It can be placed on a shelf or desk—close to where you need access to these supplies.

7. To be filed. Establish a location in your office for papers that require no additional action but just need to be filed. Don't allow this location to accumulate items that need action.

8. Names, addresses, e-mail addresses, and phone numbers. Establish a location in your office where you'll keep these pieces of information until you have time to record them in your address book. You can use either a folder that you keep close by or a small container into which you toss the information. Better yet, record it immediately and discard that piece of paper.

9. Bills. Keep bills in one location, and be sure that other family members know where this location is. You may even want to create a worksheet that lists all of the bills you pay each month, along with how much you pay and when the due date is. Look into whether you can have any of these payments automatically withdrawn from your checking account each month. If you can, you may want to add this to your worksheet as well so that you know when the money will be withdrawn from your account.

Investigate paying your bills online with your financial institution. This not only will save you money but is fast and easy. There are also bill-paying services, such as CheckFree, that you can subscribe to which will eliminate all of the paper bills you receive. You can use this service for a small fee, less than you would pay for the stamps to mail in your payments.

10. Receipts. Create a location where you'll put receipts you must keep. Whenever you get a receipt, make a decision immediately as to whether it needs to be kept (because it's a big-ticket item, a possible return, or something you must save for taxes).

You may want to keep the possible-return receipts out and close at hand in case you need to make a return. Storing these in a small container or envelope will help control unnecessary clutter. Receipts you must keep for taxes could immediately be placed in a tax folder that contains documents needed to prepare the taxes for the upcoming years. Receipts that you want to keep for major purchases you have made could be stored in an envelope, a container, or even in your filing system. In order to make retrieving them in the future easier, consider breaking down your receipts into the following categories: furniture, small appliances, large appliances, electronics, toys, clothing, jewelry, art, home decor, tools, yard, and so on. Separating your receipts into groups makes it easier to find one when you need it. Immediately toss receipts you don't need so that you don't have to spend any time looking at them later.

CHAPTER 7

CHILD'S ROOM

Children's rooms have a tendency to get messy and look disorganized due to all of the stuff kids store in their rooms, such as toys and games, books, clothes, homework, and more. Without proper storage for all of these different types of items, you can be certain it will be difficult for your child to put his or her things away so that they look neat and organized.

Aaron is the youngest of the three Cheng children and was a great sport to allow me to do an organizing makeover on his new bedroom. When I asked him why he wanted his room to be selected for my book, he looked at me with a big grin on his face and, without even thinking for a moment, said, "Because it's a mess!" Aaron also told me that he wanted to be able to have his friends over to play in his room and stay the night, but there was no space for this.

The Chengs moved into their new home shortly before Christmas 2004. Of the three children's bedrooms, Aaron's was the most appealing yet one of the most challenging spaces I've worked in. Although it didn't have a lot of extra space (its dimensions are 9¼ by 13½ feet), the ceilings were tall and had great angles, making the room look larger than it is. The other space challenge in Aaron's room was that the longest wall had a built-in sitting area running the length of the room (photos 1 and 10), which didn't leave much floor space for furniture or storage for toys. One nice feature of the room was its two full-size closets, which compensated for the shortage of floor space.

Aaron is 11 years old, so as we organized his room, we needed to take into consideration that his needs would change as he prepared for junior high and high school. Specifically, he would need an area where he could do his home-work. Finding space to put bookshelves and a desk was a challenge. As you'll read later in this chapter, we were able to maximize the use of the floor space to make room for all of the essentials that Aaron needed: a bed, bookshelves, a desk and chair, and a storage unit for toys and games. He has several different collections and is now able to view and display them all.

PROJECT BREAKDOWN	TOTAL HOURS 26.5

TASK	HOURS
Sorting, purging, and organizing	11
MaryPat and Aaron's shopping time	4
Laura's shopping time	2
Setup and installation time	8
Hauling away donations	.5
Cleanup	1
Total project time	**26.5 HOURS**

Aaron's room is the only project I completed for this book that was a complete makeover, with all new furniture and storage units. Typically I work with existing furniture and storage units in the homes I organize, and I add or subtract furniture and storage as needed. Every now and then I'll work with individuals who want to completely make over a room and are willing to eliminate all of their existing furniture and storage units. Because of this, I decided that for the book we would feature one project that was a complete makeover.

THE PROCESS

1. Dedicate time.

Aaron could hardly wait for his new room to be completed, and of course he thought it could be whipped out in a day. Unfortunately, because of the amount of work that was needed in Aaron's room, it was a process that took several days to complete.

When you tackle any organizing project, be sure to set aside enough time to work on it. In many cases, you may need to set aside time on several days to complete larger projects such as this one. Break your project into manageable

1. Their belongings have no established places or "homes," so when Mom or Dad says, "It's time to pick up your toys," the chore is overwhelming and the child doesn't know where to begin. Most kids have a toy box or a couple of big bins into which everything gets tossed. These kinds of tools make it possible to end up owning and keeping stuff past its prime. They also make it hard to access the things that kids may want to play with, engendering in them a sense that they "don't have anything to do" because they can't easily get at the toy they want.

pieces that you can realistically complete in the amount of time you've set aside.

2. Gather supplies.

To organize Aaron's room, the supplies I used initially were different from those on the standard list on page 110. They were a tape measure, a pad of paper, and an Ikea catalog. I knew I wanted to use their furniture and storage units to organize Aaron's room, so, with tape measure and paper in hand, I sketched the room's dimensions. I then discussed the needs for the room with Aaron's mom, MaryPat—everything from how to create storage for Aaron's toys, games, and books, to how to create a space where he could do his homework, and how to organize his clothes in his closet. With this understanding of Aaron's needs for his bedroom, we were able to sit down with the Ikea catalog and make an initial list of products that would help us accomplish our goals.

We also needed to ensure that all of the products we were using were going to fit in the space and that they could contain all of Aaron's belongings. Prior to beginning the organizing work, MaryPat and Aaron made a trip to Ikea to let Aaron look at furniture and storage possibilities for his room. MaryPat wanted to make sure we selected things that Aaron liked, because otherwise he would end up not using them.

3. Establish a staging area.

For Aaron's room, our staging area was located in two parts of the home, the garage and the hallway outside of Aaron's bedroom. The new furniture was stored in the garage temporarily as it was assembled, and was then moved into Aaron's bedroom—with the exception of the bed, which had to be built in his room. We used the hallway to sort books, toys, and clothes, as well as establishing an area there for donations.

For your staging area, since bedrooms are typically not that large, you'll want all the space you can find. Be sure you choose an area where you can spread out during the project, even if it means using several different temporary locations. You'll be able to see much more easily your groups of like items (the ones you'll create in step 6), which you'll eventually move back into the bedroom. Keep in mind that it's easier to see and evaluate items when they're all spread out than when they're piled up in a smaller area.

4. Sort.

Sorting through your child's belongings can be difficult, emotional, and time consuming; I've worked with several parents who were more attached to their child's toys and clothing than the child was. Children learn by the examples their parents set, though, and you are the daily role model that your child looks up to. Involving your child in this process, even if it is painful, will be one of the best things you can do for them. Helping them sort through their toys, books, games, clothes, and so on will teach excellent decision-making skills that will be beneficial all through high school, college, and adult life.

Sorting through your child's toys with them is a great opportunity to discuss the value of sharing their good fortune with others not as fortunate. Many of our clients have their children sort through their toys every year before Christmas and donate the gently used ones. This lightens their existing load as well as makes room for any new toys they may receive. Such charitable sorting can certainly take place more than

2. The storage units aren't the right type for the items that need to be kept in the bedroom.

3. The children have no established rules about cleaning up their bedrooms and putting toys and clothes in their designated areas. Some children have never had this responsibility.

4. Parents set poor examples for their children; they expect their children's rooms to be organized and picked up, yet they don't practice this behavior themselves as a model for their children.

5. The children have too much "stuff." They have things they haven't touched in months or years, but they hang on to them

continued on 102

continued from 101

because they don't know any better. These things end up shoved in the back of the closet or under the bed, never to be seen again. This then creates a foundation for more stuff to be piled or shoved in the closet or under the bed. In other words, stuff breeds stuff!

6. Children do not go through their belongings on a regular basis to find items they no longer play with or use that take up valuable space that could be used for new treasures in their rooms.

7. They hold on to toys and books past their usefulness.

once a year, and it should be encouraged so that toys continue to be rotated and used.

As you begin to sort through the contents of your child's room, consider the types of activities they're involved in. These will form the basis for the categories of items that will need to be organized. As a first pass, you may want to group all of the toys together. On the second pass, group them by type of toy, such as games, puzzles, books, action figures, blocks, balls, dolls, sporting equipment, and the like; or by collection, such as Legos, K'Nex, Polly Pockets, rocks, bottle caps, Thomas the Tank Engine, trading cards, figurines (such as horses), comic books, and so on.

In Aaron's room, we sorted his treasures into the following categories: toys, Legos, games, books, awards and trophies, clothes, sporting equipment, rock collection, art supplies, school supplies, CDs and tapes, and musical instruments.

When we examined our space during step 7, it was very easy for us to determine how much space we needed for each type of item, because we had already sorted it all out. For example, Aaron had a lot of books, so we knew he would need at least two bookshelves, which would also leave him with room to add more books in the future.

5. Purge.

Aaron didn't have an overwhelming amount of toys, games, and books in his room that we needed to sort though and purge, because some of that had already been done before the family's recent move. But we still took one quick pass through everything to see if there were any more toys we could donate or give to friends and family. As I suspected, Aaron was a trouper and filled two large bins with items to donate. He had a bit of extra motivation to let go of more things, as his mom had offered to pay him a small amount for each item he decided to donate. (I witnessed a lot of bartering between Aaron and MaryPat during the purging phase, but I think he ended up earning about $8.50 during the process!)

Purging doesn't have to be painful, and you don't need to go through the entire sorting and purging phase with your child all in one day. Break it down into manageable time segments, where you concentrate on one area for 15 or 20 minutes—or longer, if your child's attention is still going strong.

Decide early on if you plan to sell, donate, or toss the items that are no longer wanted. Be sure you have your receptacles ready and in place to sort into.

6. Group like items together.

As we sorted through the toys, games, schoolwork, memorabilia, and clothes in Aaron's room, we grouped items together in the categories we had established in step 4. MaryPat decided that some items were going to be kept elsewhere in the home, rather than in Aaron's bedroom: school memorabilia, which had a "home" in the garage; batteries, which also had a container in the garage; and some of the games, which were relocated to the family room.

We grouped together most of the remaining items, such as clothes, books, and toys. In the case of the toys, we then further grouped them by type and placed them in a bin that was later transferred to Aaron's toy storage units (photos 2 and 3).

As you're grouping toys together, you'll want to think about how frequently various toys are used and how accessible you want to make them. Grouping the same type of toys together will make it easy for your child to find the toys they want. It will also prevent them from dumping toys all over the room while looking for a certain toy, because they will be able to quickly locate that toy. If your child is old enough, involve them in this phase of the project so they'll know how the toys are grouped together.

❶

❹

❶ Aaron's room with very little floor space, including one wall that has a wall-to-wall built-in sitting area.

❷ Aaron, MaryPat, and I sorting through Aaron's toys, deciding what to keep or toss and then how to use the bins to store his different types of toys.

❸ The sorting continues—so many pieces!

❷

❸

❹ Laura moving one of the completed bins into the closet storage system.

❺ Tony and MaryPat installing the Notice board under Aaron's bed—a great place for him to make notes and post other items, such as his calendar.

❺

6 Tony and MaryPat moving the desk into its place under the bed.

7 Two free-standing bookshelves placed on top of the built-in sitting bench.

8 Aaron's two bookshelves, with space for trophies, books, and musical instruments. An extra shelf was added to help with all of the trophies and knickknacks he wanted to display. Magazine racks were used to neatly store Lego manuals.

6

9

❼

❽

❾ The desk area under the loft bed provides a cool place for Aaron to do his homework. The shelf above the desk keeps his notebooks, school supplies, and lamp off the desk, freeing up space to do homework, while the shelves to the right of the desk hold memorabilia.

❿ The hanging orange mesh bag is used to organize and store hats, balls, and other toys, and clothes are placed on open shelves in the closet for easy access.

❿

7. Examine your space.

Once you've completed the sorting and purging phase of the process, most likely you'll end up with more space to store the remaining items. It's now time to reassess your space and determine what your needs are for storing and organizing those items that will remain in the room. If your child is in elementary school, you may want to ask yourself the following questions as you begin to organize the bedroom:

▶ Will books be kept in the child's room, or will they be located in another area of the home, such as the library, family room, living room, or den?

▶ Will all of the child's toys find a home in the bedroom, or will some have a home in a family room or playroom? Which will be kept where? It's important to make these decisions up front, so you can find the perfect organizing accessories to contain the toys.

▶ Does your child use a backpack or book bag? If so, will it be returned to their room each day, or will it have an established location in a more central area of the home, such as a kitchen, laundry room, or entryway?

▶ What will be the best way for your child to keep clothes organized on a daily basis? Will it be easier to put clothes into drawers, hang them up, set them on shelves, or hang certain items on hooks on the back of the bedroom door?

▶ Will your child need a place in the room to do homework or work on craft projects?

▶ Would you like your child to have a location in the bedroom to display artwork and store schoolwork or other keepsake memorabilia?

▶ Will your child be expected to place their dirty clothes in a laundry bin in the bedroom, toss it down a laundry chute, or put it in the laundry room? If the answer is "in the bedroom," be sure to provide a bin or basket; otherwise, you may find it on the floor instead.

Once you've asked yourself these questions and looked at the quantity of items you have in each category, you should have a good general idea of the type of products you need. Now you can start to create your shopping list. Be sure to take into account the room and closet dimensions.

In Aaron's room, after we asked ourselves the above questions, it was quite simple to flip through the Ikea catalog and make a shopping list that fit our needs. Aaron had his own ideas about how his room should look, of course, and we used many of them.

Because floor space was at a premium, we had to maximize the space yet still incorporate furniture and storage based on Aaron's needs. In the original layout, most of Aaron's floor space was consumed by his bed (photo 1). This left little room for anything else. We decided to give Aaron a loft bed, which freed up most of his floor space, thus giving us more room for a desk and toy storage.

8. Shop!

Shopping—for many people, it's the best part of organizing. It truly is a nice reward for your hard work and a job well done. And even if you don't enjoy shopping, everyone loves to receive something new—even your children. At the beginning of your organizing project, spend some time with your child to discuss the rewards of organizing. In this case, the reward will be the opportunity to receive new items for their room that will help them keep their toys nice and neat.

Encourage them to shop with you and let you know what products they'd like to use to keep their toys organized. After all, it just makes sense to involve them in the selection process if it helps them get their toys and other possessions into those areas when it's pickup time. Remember that it has to be fun and simple!

Aaron had a great time shopping and getting the opportunity to help select some of the products for his room. He also got to choose many of the colors

PRODUCT LIST

STORE	ITEM/SERVICE	SIZE	COST	TOTAL $
Ikea	Stolmen full/double loft bed frame			249.00
	Vika Amon (white desk)	47½" w × 29½" H		19.00
	Vika Curry (silver legs for desk)			20.00
	Billy bookshelves (white)	31½" w × 11" D × 14¾" H	2 × 59.00	118.00
	Extra shelf for bookshelf			12.00
	Trofast (toy storage w/pull-out bins)	17⅜" w × 11¾" D × 35⅞" H	2 × 59.00	118.00
	Pull-out bins for Trofast storage	4" high	4 × 2.00	8.00
		9" high	4 × 3.00	12.00
	Jarpen (white shelf)	46⅞" w × 11" D		9.99
	Bjarnum (brackets for white shelf)			10.00
	Lack (white shelves)	43¼" w × 10¼" D	2 × 14.99	29.98
	Bits magnetic board (white)	16" w × 23" H		6.99
	Kludd notice board			16.99
	Trean (wall spotlight lamp)			5.99
	PS Fangst (hanging storage bag)			7.99
	Two-bar magnetic rack		2 × .99	1.98
	Knuff (magazine holders)		3 × 2.99	8.97
	Mackis (CD storage unit)			12.99
	Morker (white desk lamp)			4.99
	Dokument (silver wastepaper basket)			4.99
	Ringum (gray pile rug)			34.99
	Skruvsta (black swivel desk chair)			129.00
	Helmer (six-drawer unit)	11" w × 16¾" D × 27⅛" H		49.99
			total	891.83
Other stores	Chrome basket			7.00
	Hooks for coats and backpacks			10.00
			total	17.00
			TOTAL COST OF CHILD'S ROOM PRODUCTS	**$908.83**

of the products. Because he actively participated in the process, he was much more willing and able to maintain what his mom and I created for him—not to mention that he now has an ultra-cool room to show all of his friends!

We had a pretty good idea of the products we needed before we even went to the store. Because we had looked in the catalog and taken measurements, we were able to come up with a list to work from and then review our selections once we got there. We ended up changing our minds about a few of the products, but our list gave us a very good start. All of the products we used in Aaron's bedroom are listed on the previous page.

9. Install products.

Installing products for this project took on a whole new meaning. We had a lot of furniture to assemble, which took several hours: the bed, the desk, two bookshelves, and two toy storage units. Due to its size, the bed was constructed in the bedroom, whereas the other, smaller pieces of furniture were assembled in the garage and then moved into place in Aaron's room.

Bed: We chose a loft bed for Aaron's room, which basically doubled his floor space. This enabled us to create an area where he could do his homework, which was one of the goals of our project (photo 9).

White desk: The desk provided a large work surface where Aaron could do his homework and other projects without feeling cramped (photo 9).

Bookshelves: These were used for more than just books. We used a few shelves to display Aaron's trophies, special rocks, and other keepsakes. The top of one of the shelves was used to store musical instruments that he didn't use often. We also added an extra shelf, which enabled us to display Aaron's knickknacks without having to cram them onto just one shelf and the top of the bookshelf (photos 7 and 8).

Toy storage units with pull-out bins: These two units housed the majority of Aaron's toys, again grouped by category. The great thing about these units is that Aaron can take out a bin and play with the contents, and when he's done, he can just scoop them back up and slide the bin back into the wood frame. We sorted the toys directly into the bins (photos 2 and 3), which were later placed in the wood frames. Having these bins to help us with the sorting kept all of our piles of toys organized.

Installing the three shelves next to Aaron's desk, the magnetic board, the notice board, the wall spotlight lamp, the mesh hanging storage bag, the magnetic racks, the chrome basket, and the hooks for coats and backpacks was also part of this phase. With these products, happily, we didn't need to assemble them before they were installed.

White shelf: This shelf was installed above Aaron's desk to hold frequently used items such as his CDs, lamp, school notebooks stored in one of the magazine holders, and various school supplies (photo 9).

White shelves: These were placed at arm's length to the right of Aaron's desk and used to display photos, some of his rock collection, religious statues, and other keepsakes. There's room for Aaron to display additional items, and he can look at them while he is at his desk (photo 9).

Magnetic board: This was installed above the hooks for the coats and used to display photos and other items to take back to school (photo 10).

Notice board: This was installed to the right of Aaron's desk as a place for him to write notes as well as to hold his calendar and other notices and cards he received (photo 9).

Mesh hanging storage bag: This bag provided colorful compartmentalized storage for Aaron's baseball hats, small balls, and card decks (photo 10).

Chrome basket: This was attached to Aaron's bed with cable ties in order to hold his books, flashlight, and water bottle, as seen in the photo at the beginning of the chapter.

Hooks for coats and backpacks: MaryPat expected Aaron to hang his coats and backpack in his closet, but she quickly learned that this wasn't realistic. She decided that hooks on the wall would be the best solution, and the simplest for Aaron to maintain on a daily basis (photo 10).

When you're getting ready to do your installation, you'll want to make sure that you have all of the hardware you need, so that you don't need to keep running to the store. In MaryPat's case, she needed both drywall and wood screws, but didn't have the wood screws, so that meant one more trip to the store.

In some organizing projects, all you may need to do at the installation phase is to simply put the new products in place and fill them with the items they're intended to organize. For example, in Aaron's room, we used one magazine holder to contain his notebooks on the shelf above his desk, and we stored all of his Lego instructions in another magazine holder and placed that on his bookshelf (photo 8). The CD storage unit, desk lamp, wastepaper basket, rug, desk chair, and Helmer six-drawer unit also simply needed to be set in place. The six-drawer unit was placed under Aaron's desk to conserve floor space, and was used to keep his school supplies and coin collection organized.

We had originally contemplated having custom bookshelves built on either side of Aaron's window to hold books, toys, and trophies. As we talked further about this idea, however, we realized that it wasn't the best solution. We determined that the bed we were going to use would end up hiding one of the shelves, and that it would be much simpler, not to mention more cost effective, to place two bookshelves on top of the window ledge (photos 7 and 10).

In the future, this solution will also allow the Chengs to convert the room to suit another purpose, without having to worry about what to do with the custom-built shelves. The blank wall that's not really usable for storage is going to be the site of a poster collage instead. The collage will be extended around the room in the space under the loft, to create a wallpaper effect. Aaron love's posters, and this will put them where he can actually enjoy them. The poster collage is an idea the Chengs came up with after we completed the project.

Because we didn't address every aspect of the room, it left them some space to be inspired!

10. Maintain.

When our project was complete, Aaron couldn't believe the amount of space he had. Even I was surprised. "I can keep my room clean now because I have so much space," Aaron told me. "And it'll be easier to find my stuff!"

Maintaining the organizing systems we created should be pretty simple for Aaron. When his mom asks him to clean up his room, he should have no problem doing so because he now has a place for everything. Not only that, he has additional storage space that we didn't use. One final maintenance step for Aaron will be going through the toys and other items in his room at least a few times a year to determine what he's no longer using or playing with. If Aaron doesn't do this, he will eventually run out of space.

CHILD'S ROOM ORGANIZING TIPS

1. Start young. Establish a time or times each day when your children are to pick up their toys and put them in their designated areas. (Be sure they have a designated area for the items you're asking them to pick up, or they'll become frustrated with this task.) This is what we refer to as maintenance. Even a toddler can put their blocks into a bin. This exercise can be introduced as a game when the child is young and will ideally become part of the daily routine.

2. Establish a designated area for certain items, such as backpacks, homework, coats, shoes, paperwork to take back to school, lunch box, and library books. Make sure your child knows where this location is so that these items aren't strewn throughout your home, beginning at the door they came in through.

3. Allow your child to sell their toys and books. There are bookstores that will buy used books, and your child can use the money to purchase new ones. If you have a garage sale, allow your child to have their own table of items to sell. Provide them with special stickers, and help them mark their sale items. Then show them how much money they earned, which they can use to purchase a new toy or add to their savings account.

4. Organize by example. Take a look around your home. Are you setting a good example for your child to keep their room organized and picked up?

5. What is the goal of the organizing? This is key to keep in mind. If the goal is to keep the clothes off the bedroom floor, does it really matter whether they're kept shoved in drawers, hung, or stuffed into wire baskets? Even if you like a system, your children may not maintain it. Determine what you're willing to tolerate—and even then, you may need to compromise.

MaryPat told me she had to accept that her sense of "organized" was not the same as that of her middle child, Catherine. The two recently negotiated about Catherine's room. MaryPat gave in about requiring that everything be picked up and put away on a consistent basis, and Catherine agreed to segregate her dirty clothes from her clean ones and keep garbage out of her room. MaryPat believes this is something they can both live with. (If Catherine doesn't keep her end of the bargain, of course, then she has to do it MaryPat's way!)

When asked, Aaron told me that the best part of his entire room is the new bed. Although we wouldn't traditionally think of a bed as an organizing product, in this case it was one of our biggest space-savers. We were able to put Aaron's desk, shelves, six-drawer unit, and chair under the bed, freeing up much floor space (photo 9).

I checked in on Aaron's room a couple of months after we completed the project. It had remained amazingly organized! He was doing his homework in his room every day now that he had a space to work. After the project was complete, Aaron got a stereo for his room, and he even had plenty of space for it.

Aaron now has a bedroom that he can be proud of, one that he couldn't wait to show his friends. I couldn't have been more thrilled with how the room turned out, and was very pleased that Aaron worked with both his mom and me to find a solution for his room's chaos.

CHAPTER 8

LAUNDRY ROOM

The laundry room is one of those spaces in your house that can become a catchall for just about anything that does not have a "home." Each room in your home serves a purpose—sometimes more than one. Deciding the purpose of your laundry room is an excellent place to start organizing. Obviously, the main purpose of the laundry room is as a place to wash and dry your clothes. In most cases, laundry rooms or closets can serve additional purposes, such as a place to hang clothes, store cleaning supplies, act as a mud room, house your pet's food dish and/or litter box . . . the list goes on.

The amount of space you have in your laundry room will help you determine just how many purposes this room can serve. As with any organizing project, if you create "homes" for things you need to store in the laundry room, it will help you keep it from being an area where things just pile up!

The laundry room was the final project I chose for this book. It was also the most difficult to choose. I saw just about everything imaginable—from rooms that looked like they didn't need any help, to rooms that looked like a bomb had gone off and clothes and other items had gone flying through the air.

There are so many styles of laundry rooms: laundry closets, laundry rooms in garages, laundry rooms that double as utility rooms or pantries, laundry rooms that have stackable washer and dryers, and laundry rooms that you pass through from the garage into the house.

My hope was to find a laundry room that was in a home, with a washer and dryer side by side, that didn't need an "extreme makeover," but rather just needed to make better use of its existing space with a little help from some organizing products designed especially for the laundry room. In the end, it was my friend Melinda who volunteered her laundry room.

MELINDA'S STORY

Melinda has always offered her home to me for any organizing project I needed to do. I've known her since college and don't view her as disorganized, so it was hard for me to understand why she would want to offer me her laundry room for the book. But I told her to send me photos of the room, including the insides of the cabinets, so that I could get a better understanding of what we would need to do to eliminate her chaos in this area.

Melinda's laundry room is your typical laundry room. You pass through it from the garage when entering the house. The main purposes her laundry room serves are to wash and dry clothes; store laundry-related items; hang coats, backpacks, and bags; store cleaning supplies and light bulbs; and store the iron and ironing board. It's also a place to put the incoming and outgoing mail and to store a few additional odds and ends. The laundry room is pretty much Melinda's domain, and it drives her crazy because although she can find everything she needs, she still feels that it's cluttered when she opens the cabinet doors and looks at the top of the cabinets (photo 1).

Melinda and I spent a little over an hour on the phone going over the contents of each cabinet, as well as what was stored on top of the cabinets. She explained to me in detail what worked, what wasn't working, what she liked,

PROJECT BREAKDOWN — TOTAL HOURS (19)

TASK	HOURS
Sorting, purging, and organizing	10
Melinda's shopping time (online & in stores)	5
Laura's shopping time (online & in stores)	1.5
Installation time	1.5
Hauling away donations	1
Total project time	**19 HOURS**

and what was driving her nuts. I asked her some questions about items that seemed out of place in the laundry room—such as a broken game on top of the cabinet, which just needed to be fixed; a foot soaker and massager; and her old maternity clothes. Several other items just needed to be eliminated, she indicated, since she was no longer using them. (I agreed—of course!) The remaining items needed to call the laundry room home.

We discussed how we could make the best use of the space by reorganizing some of the areas, with the help of organizing products designed for the laundry room. I directed Melinda to a number of Web sites offering laundry room organizing products, and asked her to tell me which products she thought she would like to use to help her maximize the space. A day later we reviewed her product selections and discussed in great detail exactly what we would do to her laundry room.

THE PROCESS

1. Dedicate time.

Melinda and I were determined to complete her laundry room overhaul in less than a day. We succeeded, partly due to her mom, who took care of Melinda's two young boys, ages five and three, for the day so we could focus on the project. Another major contributor to our success was Rob, who installed products for us during a good part of the day.

If you have young children and are serious about completing an organizing project in a short amount of time without distractions, consider enlisting the help of a friend, family member, or sitter. It will allow you the opportunity to stay focused and provide you with the peace of mind and sense of accomplishment that comes with completing what you begin.

2. Gather supplies.

As with most organizing projects, the necessary supplies for Melinda's laundry room overhaul consisted of a garbage can, recycling bins, and boxes or garbage bags to use for sorting.

This project, like our child's room (see chapter 7), was different from most in that we decided quite early in the project, during this phase, which organizing products we would buy. As previously mentioned, Melinda and I spent a lot of time on the phone dissecting each cabinet and the surfaces in her laundry room to determine what we would be removing and how we could best use the space. By doing this, we were able to come up with a list of products to purchase, which appears in step 8 (shop).

With most projects, I find it close to impossible to shop up front. That's because I never know what will be eliminated, what will be kept but moved to another room, and what will be kept in that area and need to be organized.

3. Establish a staging area.

Melinda's laundry room was located near the family room, with a hallway that ran between the two rooms. We used both the hallway and the family room as staging areas for sorting as well as for garbage. We also used the hallway to group by category the items that Melinda wanted to keep and put back into the laundry room (photo 4).

Most laundry rooms are so short on space that you'll want to determine a location you can use for sorting while you're organizing the room. This could be a hallway, another room, or even the garage, depending on how close it is to the laundry room.

FOUR COMMON PROBLEMS OF LAUNDRY ROOMS

1. Laundry rooms become a catchall storage area for items that don't have a home.

2. There isn't enough space to hang-dry clothes.

3. There isn't enough horizontal space to fold clothes.

4. There is limited space to put dirty clothes.

4. Sort.

For Melinda's laundry room, we did two rounds of sorting. We completed the first round while talking on the phone and looking at photos of her laundry room. During that round, we identified several items that needed to be removed and relocated to other areas of her home (photo 3) and many others that just needed to be thrown away. The second round of sorting happened on the day that I worked with her at her home. We moved almost everything from her laundry room into our staging area, and came up with the following categories: coats; backpacks and bags; ironing supplies; cleaning supplies; laundry supplies; light bulbs; extension cords; clothes that needed stains removed; brooms and mops; stepstool; cell phone cords and chargers; and painting clothes for the boys.

By placing the baskets and bins we had on hand for the project in the hallway, we were able to sort directly into these containers (photo 4). Some of the containers ended up being too small, as they started to fill up rather quickly, so we just transferred the contents to a larger container until we had the correct sizes for those items we were attempting to store.

5. Purge.

Although Melinda's laundry room was the smallest project completed for the book, that didn't mean she didn't have things to purge. Here are some of the items she discarded: extra phone cords, lots of extra rags, plastic bags from sheets (which she had thought she might store something in), coatrack, plastic bins that didn't match, sweater drying rack (kept one, discarded one), folding wood drying rack, Halloween costume packaging, shelf paper, cloth laundry bags, three plastic laundry bins, and empty shoeboxes.

As mentioned earlier, Melinda had decided there were a number of items in the laundry room that didn't need to be stored there. This illustrates problem number one of laundry rooms—they often end up becoming a catchall for items that don't have a home. In Melinda's case, these items included maternity clothes, games, framed photos, foot soaker and massager (now stored in the bathroom), wicker silverware basket holder, and Christmas drinking glasses in their box (photo 3). Melinda's laundry room also held drying racks for sweaters. You would think that would be the right place for them, but in reality, Melinda didn't have room to dry her sweaters on the racks. She did have room upstairs in the bedroom, so it made more sense to store them in the linen closet upstairs.

As you organize your laundry room, it's important to be specific about what you want to store in this room and stick to that plan, so that the room doesn't become the "catchall" room.

6. Group like items together.

When organizing any room, create a list of the categories of items that will be kept there. Then group like items together. Grouping allows you to realistically determine how much space you'll need in the room to store each type of item. It will also help you when you get to the next two steps, which are to examine your space and to shop.

In Melinda's laundry room, we grouped items into the categories we established in step 4 as we were removing things from the laundry room.

7. Examine your space.

Melinda and I examined the space in her laundry room on two separate occasions. The first time was over the phone, when I looked at photos of her room, and the second time was when I was at her home, working on the project. The first time we examined the space, I started a list of products that I thought could help her make better use of her space. Some of my ideas that may also work well in your laundry room include the following:

◆ Use turntables for cleaning and laundry supplies in cabinets instead of just placing them on shelves. When items are placed on shelves, they have a tendency to get shoved to the back, and it's difficult to see what you have (photo 12).

❶ Stuff jammed into all of the cupboards and lying around on the counter, washer, and tops of cabinets—creating one big headache for Melinda.

❷ The fun is just beginning as we start to pull everything out of the cabinets and sort it into groups of like items.

❸ After our initial sort we determined that several items in the laundry room no longer needed to call it home. Some of these included maternity clothes, a foot soaker, a picture, baby items, Christmas glasses, and more. These items were all relocated to other areas of the house.

❸

❹

❻

❹ Items were grouped together in new wicker baskets and plastic bins as we pulled them from the laundry room to sort. We ended up with baskets and bins for each of the following groups of like items: felt pads for chairs, light bulbs, clothes for art projects, clothes to be mended, various adapters, and extension cords.

❺ Turntables aren't just for the kitchen—they work great in the laundry room as well, allowing easy access to laundry and cleaning supplies.

❻ Melinda placing cleaning rags on a pull-out shelf in a very narrow and odd-sized cabinet. Being able to pull out the shelf will make it much easier for her to find what she is looking for in this very small cabinet.

⑦ Using two rows of hooks behind the door instead of one allows more of the wall to be utilized. They should be placed at heights so that clothing does not touch the floor.

⑧ Pull-out bins, shelves, or, in this case, a pot-lid organizer are used to store frequently used cleaning supplies under the sink, so that they don't all get shoved to the back of the cabinet.

⑨ A cookie jar in the laundry room? Yes—it's a fun and decorative way to store laundry detergent.

9

10

10 Over-the-door holders keep ironing boards hidden and out of the way. Many include a place to store an iron and even a bottle of spray starch or linen spray. Hooks for coats on the wall behind the door help to keep the space free of clutter. Use individual hooks that screw into the wall for brooms and maps. The white two-bin wall organizer is great for outgoing and incoming mail—and is a handy place to hang keys.

11 No floor space for drying sweaters? Consider a wall-mounted pull-out rack.

12 Beautifully organized cabinets—it's so easy to see everything! The shelves in the right cabinet were adjusted from the bottom up to ensure enough space for items on each shelf. Bins on the shelves provide a clean look, but also make it easy to contain items and get to everything at once. Use decorative baskets on the tops of cabinets to store additional items while eliminating visible clutter.

12

- Use an over-the-door holder for the ironing board, and perhaps the iron and spray bottles as well (photo 10).

- Attach a drying rack to the wall that extends to allow clothes to hang dry (photo 11).

- Use multiple coat hooks behind a door to keep coat and backpack clutter out of sight (photo 7).

- Use individual hooks behind the door to hang brooms and mops. Using individual hooks and staggering them allows you to hang more things in a small area than if you installed just one vertical hook that hung four or five items (photo 10).

- Use pull-out drawers to store cleaning supplies in cabinets, so you can see everything you have—all the way to the back of the cabinets (photos 6 and 8).

- Where you have space on top of cabinets, use baskets to hide and contain items. It will give the room a cleaner look (photo 12).

8. Shop!

I always recommend that you sort, purge, and group similar items together before you shop for products. You want to purchase products that will work in the space you have and that will contain the items you're keeping. For Melinda's project, as I mentioned, we actually did most of the shopping before I went to her house to work on the room. I did this because we had already spent several hours on the phone discussing in detail what would be eliminated, what would be moved to other areas of the house, and what would be left that needed to be organized. Because I had a very clear idea of the items to be organized, we were able to create our product list and shop, so that when I arrived at her home to work on the room, I had the products I needed and we were able to complete the project in one afternoon.

PRODUCT LIST

STORE	ITEM/SERVICE	SIZE	COST	TOTAL $
	Expandable wall clothes drying rack			21.99
	Maple/chrome coatracks		2 × 27.99	55.98
	Rope baskets	medium	3 × 21.99	65.97
	Rum stripe baskets		set of 3	79.99
Organize-Everything.com	*Twin pump soap and lotion dispenser (stainless steel)*			24.99
	Scented hand soap			10.99
	Mini stepstool			34.95
	Scented ironing spray			15.99
	Scented laundry detergent			17.99
			total	328.84
	Two-bin organizer			19.98
Lillian Vernon	*Pot lid organizer*			14.98
	White slide-out organizer			12.98
	Poppy print ironing board cover			14.98
			total	62.92
	Glass cookie jar			19.95
	Hooks for brooms			2.49
Other Organizing Stores	*Turntables*		2 × 3.95	7.90
	Plastic bins		4 × 2.95	11.80
	Screws			6.79
	Over-the-door ironing board holder			9.99
			total	58.92
		TOTAL OF LAUNDRY ROOM PRODUCTS		**$450.68**

This project was one of the more difficult ones to shop for, because there was a very limited amount of space to work with and a lot of things that needed to be kept in the room. The lower cabinets were also extremely narrow and on an angle, making it very challenging to use the space (photos 1 and 6). We invested almost as much time in finding just the right products as we spent actually working in the laundry room.

9. Install products.

During this project, we had two types of products to install: those that needed to be screwed into the walls and into cabinets in order to be used, and loose products, such as bins and turntables, that just needed to be set in place. Rob served as my handyman for the day while Melinda's husband was at work. He helped us with the products that had to be physically installed:

Two-bin organizer: This was used for holding mail and keys (photo 10). Melinda's laundry room was located next to the garage, and she would place a lot of things there and then later disperse them to the rest of the house. Before, the mail used to pile up on either the counter or the top of the washer or dryer.

Expandable wall clothes drying rack: Melinda had very little space to hang clothes that needed to be dried. She had one rod above the sink, but when she hung clothes from it, it was difficult to use the sink. The wall drying rack (photo 11) gave her extra space for hanging items to dry; once they were dry, the rack could just be pushed back to the wall and out of the way, thus taking up very little space.

Maple/chrome coatracks: These two racks were used for coats, bags, and backpacks (photo 7). They were installed only after determining the heights of the different items that would be hung on each rack. We knew we would use the bottom rack for backpacks and the boys' coats, which are shorter. Before installing the two coat racks on the wall behind the door, Rob needed to measure to ensure that coats and backpacks did not end up dragging on the floor. To do this, we gathered all of the short hanging items, such as the kids' coats and backpacks, then selected the longest coat and hung it from the rack with the rack laid up against the wall, so we could mark the spot where the holes were to be drilled. After that coat rack was installed, we gathered the adults' coats and, again, selected the longest one to hang on the rack with it resting up against the wall so we could mark the spot for the holes to be drilled. This ensured that the adults' coats would not cover the kids' coats (photo 10).

Hooks for brooms (photo 10).

Pot-lid organizer: This was used to hold cleaning supplies under the sink (photo 8).

White slide-out organizer: This was used for rags, mop pads, and sponges (photo 6).

The remaining products just needed to be set in place with the items we pre-determined for each. Most of the products we used were self-explanatory, with the exception of the ones below:

Glass cookie jar: This jar was used to give Melinda easy and quick access to the powdered clothes detergent (photo 9). Previously, she had a large box of detergent under the sink, with things piled on top of it. It was awkward to get at the soap from underneath the counter. Placing the filled cookie jar on the counter next to the washing machine not only looked nice but was also much more functional.

Rope baskets and rum stripe baskets: We used these to contain items in various places, such on top of the cabinets (photo 12). The rope baskets looked much more stylish on top of Melinda's cabinets than the loose items that had been scattered there. Two of the rope baskets were used to store light bulbs, thus freeing up a lot of cabinet space. Light bulbs aren't used that often, and they were taking up a lot of Melinda's precious cabinet space that could have been better used by items she needed to get to every day. The third rope basket was used to hold painting shirts for the boys, paintbrushes, and a mat for painting. Two of the rum stripe baskets replaced her old plastic colored laundry baskets that didn't match each other (photo 11). They also helped to brighten up the laundry room. The third rum stripe basket was used to hold those items that came into the house from the car when Melinda got home. Previously, she would have just placed these items on the counter in the laundry room or on top of the washer or dryer. Now she has a place to contain them until she has a few minutes to put them in their proper places.

10. Maintain.

Now that Melinda's laundry room is completely organized, her challenge will be to keep it that way. In the past, Melinda had a tendency to store things in the laundry room when she wasn't sure where to put them in the house. I don't think that Melinda will do this anymore, as I know how much she loves the new look of her laundry room. Having the rum stripe basket for those items that need to be dispersed to the rest of the home will also help her on a daily basis. The key here is to take a few minutes each day to put things in their designated areas.

Overall, Melinda's laundry room was not what I'd consider to be an extreme laundry room makeover. She didn't have piles of stuff everywhere or tons of stuff that she didn't need. Rather, Melinda's challenge was to determine how to best use her space, with the assistance of some new products that could help her maximize her space and eliminate the clutter she saw when she opened her cabinets. Mission accomplished. In addition, Melinda ended up with several nice decorative touches as well, which helped to brighten the room.

LAUNDRY ROOM ORGANIZING TIPS

The following tips are provided courtesy of Jennifer Humes. See the "Shopping Resources" appendix for more about Jennifer's products and services.

1. Delegate responsibility. When it comes to doing the laundry and keeping the room organized, delegate some responsibilities to other family members rather than trying to do it all yourself. Walk them through the process of doing the laundry, including how to treat stains and hand-wash delicates.

2. Streamline and upgrade your appliances. A stackable washer and dryer requires less room, therefore creating additional space.

3. Simplify the sorting process with color-coded pop-up hampers that are snag-free.

4. Use a separate hamper to collect clothes that need to be dry-cleaned.

5. If space is limited, add shelving above doors, in corners, and above the washer and dryer.

6. Use an over-the-door ironing board if space is limited (photo 10).

7. Use an accordion drying rack. It's retractable and easy to store.

8. Use an over-the-door pocket organizer to provide additional storage in a previously unused space.

9. Post stain guides and reference information on cabinet doors.

10. Designate one area for folding laundry using a stand-alone folding table or a wall-mounted folding rack.

11. If you store things up high, keep a stepstool or ladder nearby.

12. Make a list of what you have and what you need. Maintaining a list of the things you use makes it easier to know when you need to replenish. Buying in bulk isn't always cost-effective, especially if you don't have the storage space.

13. Brighten the space by painting walls, replacing light bulbs with a higher wattage, or using stylish storage products (photo 11).

14. Store frequently used items within reach and less frequently used items up higher. Keep laundry soap near the washer (photo 9), hangers near the dryer (photo 12), and spray starch near the ironing board.

15. Use a permanent marker or label maker to clearly label containers.

CHAPTER 9

GARAGE

Does the thought of your garage make you nauseated? Is there so much stuff in your garage that you feel overwhelmed and you don't know where to begin? Has your garage become the dumping ground of your house? If you're saying "yes" to any of these questions, then I hope this chapter inspires you to take action and change the way you look at your garage on a daily basis.

Before we get started, though, I'd like you to contemplate the following important question: What purpose would you like your garage to serve? Once you have the answer to this question, you can begin the process of creating the desired space and organizing your garage.

There are many uses for the garage, some of which might include storage, workshop, personal gym, play area for children, office, parking, or a combination of the above. After you've decided how you want to use the space in your garage, you're ready to begin the process of turning it into a functional area.

If you're like most people, the garage is the last room of the house you see as you leave for work in the morning and the first room you see when you arrive home, regardless of whether you actually park your car in the garage. Whether or not you're aware of it, the clutter that you see at least twice a day remains in your subconscious, eating away at you because you know you should do something about it.

Think for a moment about the fact that this is the one room of the house to which many people leave the door wide open—for all of the neighbors to see! Yikes!!! Regardless of whether your entire house or just the garage is filled with clutter, you might be giving the wrong impression to your neighbors and the people driving by who can look into your garage and see the piles of stuff. In most cases, the garage is the messiest and most disorganized room in the home and is not a true representation of the rest of the home, so why let your neighbors look at it?

THE CHENGS' STORY

As with each of the projects that were selected for this book, the Cheng family has their own unique story to tell. It's one that most people will encounter at least once in their life, if not several times. One month prior to when I put out a call for projects for this book, the Chengs—MaryPat, Tony, and their three children, Madeline, 18, Catherine, 15, and Aaron, 11—moved into a new home. It was just a couple of weeks before Christmas, and they had boxes everywhere in their two-car garage. Some of the boxes contained items that still needed to be unpacked and put in the house, but most of the items needed a location in the garage.

The Chengs agreed that the purpose their two-car garage was going to serve would be to provide a parking place for both of their cars. They hadn't had a garage at their previous home and were eager to have a place to park. I was excited to work with the Chengs because they didn't want their garage to be just a storage unit for their stuff; rather, they wanted to start out on the right foot shortly after moving in and get their garage organized so they could park their cars there right away during the winter months.

So often I encounter families who move into a new home, move all of their boxes into the garage, and then fail to get the boxes unpacked or find a permanent location in the garage where they can be kept. This makes it impossible

PROJECT BREAKDOWN — TOTAL HOURS (51)

TASK	HOURS
Sorting, purging, and organizing	39
Additional sorting time	6
MaryPat's shopping time	2
Installation time	3
Hauling away donations	1
Total project time	**51** HOURS

FIVE COMMON PROBLEMS OF GARAGES

1. The "I'll just toss it in the garage" approach leads to a garage in which it's close to impossible to find anything.

2. The clutter becomes so over-whelming that you have no idea how to make the space func-tional and organized.

3. Valuable cars that are used every day have to park outside the garage because so much useless junk is being stored in there.

4. You waste time looking for things you know you have, but can't locate.

5. Animals make their homes in your garage among your card-board boxes.

to ever park a car in the garage. Over a period of time, it becomes more and more acceptable to simply toss something into the garage with everything else—just to get it out of the way, never to be looked at or dealt with again. The Chengs had already begun to develop this nasty habit shortly after they moved into their new home: a few empty pizza boxes had been tossed into the garage, on their way to the recycling bins outside.

THE PROCESS

1. Dedicate time.

As with any organizing project, time needs to be scheduled in order to accomplish the task at hand. We blocked off an entire Sunday to get the Chengs' project started. Both parents were home from work with no phone interruptions or meetings, and the children were all home from school, thus enabling this project to be a family affair. It was important to MaryPat and Tony to engage all of their children in this project so that they would take ownership of their work and help maintain the garage after it was organized. MaryPat didn't want sole responsibility for deciding which sporting equipment was kept and which was discarded; which old toys got to stay and which went to younger nieces and nephews; and, finally, which memorabilia meant something to anyone else besides herself!

Keep in mind that maintenance is step 10 of our process, and it's something all family members need to participate in. Engaging children at the beginning of the process so they feel a part of the creation of the system will help to ensure participation over the years in maintaining what they've worked hard to create. In the case of the Chengs, this strategy also served to "police" maintenance. If any one member of the family messed things up, or didn't clean up after using the garage or its contents, other family members quickly reminded them to do so.

TIP

What days are you going to work on your garage? Schedule them on your calendar so that you make an appointment with yourself to get the job done. Resist the urge to say you'll do it "someday"—it will never get done this way.

2. Gather supplies.

See the list on page 154 for the supplies you'll need. We used five old moving boxes to place things the Chengs would not be keeping, which we labeled as follows: trash, donate, give to family and friends, garage sale, and eBay or consign (photo 5).

In most cases, I'm not in favor of shopping for products until step 8. For this project, I made an exception and worked with MaryPat to purchase several different sizes of plastic bins to transfer items into for consistent, safe, and dry storage. We left all other shopping for step 8.

3. Establish a staging area.

Because it's close to impossible to complete the next three steps of the project without having adequate space to work in, you'll want to create a staging area where you can place things as you begin to sort through them.

At the Cheng home, we used the covered carport area (photos 4 and 5). Here we placed our boxes for items that were leaving the garage (read "purging") as well as boxes for groups of similar items that were to be put back in the garage. The Chengs and I were very fortunate to have this covered work area as a staging area, especially since they live in Bellevue, a suburb of Seattle, where it's known to rain on occasion. If you don't have a covered carport, a driveway or even the front lawn will work.

The important thing is that you want enough space so that you aren't tripping over things as you work. You want to be able to see the separation of categories of items that you'll be keeping. Don't risk breaking a foot, as I've done

1

1 The results of moving in and needing to find a place for everything, including two cars! Breaking down boxes instantly frees up a lot of space.

2 So many things, so little space! We will find a home for all of these items before we finish organizing the garage.

3 Madeline and Tony removing the bulky furniture from the garage so we could get to the boxes in the back.

4 Aaron sorting his toys. He donated several and earned a little spending cash for a new toy.

4

5

2

3

5 Our receptacles for donations and sale items are ready to be put to good use for no-longer-needed items. Close by was our designated area for groups of items that belong in the garage.

6 Madeline sorting through hundreds of ballet shoes.

7 What does being disorganized cost? We found a check for $3,292.14 that could no longer be cashed.

8 A look of shock after finding the "the check"!

6

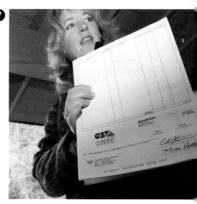

7

8

GARAGE

141

9

11

9 After all items were sorted and grouped together into bins, they were placed back in the garage until the shelving units could be installed.

10 After the narrow wood shelves were removed, new deep and tall shelves were set in place for maximum storage.

11 Onrax hanging shelving was installed to store holiday decor.

12 Sporting equipment stored along the back wall and not far from the door that goes to the backyard. We needed to find a storage location for the large rolling recycling and trash bins that provided easy access to the door leading into the house. The workbench was left in place for future projects and storage. Rubbermaid paint containers were placed on shelves above the workbench for quick access. The minivan will fit in front of the recycling bins.

12

GARAGE

143

in the past, by tripping over something in your garage because you didn't allow yourself enough space to work in.

4. Sort.

Now the real work begins! After doing an initial assessment of what existed at a high level in the garage, we came up with the following categories of items that the Cheng garage contained: kids' keepsake clothes, kids' keepsake blankets, kids' keepsake toys and toys for guests to play with, beach blankets and toys, sports equipment (including a newly acquired Ping-Pong table, which they wanted to store in its collapsed form), memorabilia, Christmas decorations, Halloween decorations, Easter decorations, crafts, computer accessories, gardening supplies and chemicals, tools, paint supplies, luggage, refrigerator and freezer, and trash and recycling bins.

We designated areas under the carport and in the driveway for each of these categories. We labeled each area to make it easier for the Chengs' children to place things in the appropriate temporary area (photo 5).

Sometimes the hardest part of the organizing process is knowing where to start. In this case, we started at the front of the garage on one side and worked our way through the room (photo 1). With each item we touched or box that we looked in, we decided what category it would fall in and placed it in that designated location. We did this with everything that was in the garage until it was nearly empty. Some of the boxes we looked in contained things that could fall in many categories and thus would need some "fine sorting," but we saved that until we were finished with our initial pass through the garage. By doing this cursory first pass, we were quickly able to assess how much stuff was in a particular category.

After our initial sort, with the garage nearly empty, we determined that the Christmas decorations, memorabilia, and children's keepsake clothes, blankets, and toys were the categories that were going to require the most space. We needed to keep this in mind when we planned the space in the garage for each of our categories.

Now it was time to do some fine sorting, and every-one participated. In the fine sorting phase, each family member took boxes of their treasures and went through them, making many tough decisions about what would be donated, thrown away, given to friends and family, or sold. It wasn't all hard work and no play, though, as I heard lots of laughter about what they were finding. You may note that our fine sorting process was transitioning into the purging process, which is our next step. Some-times these two steps go hand in hand and can be done at the same time.

TIP

Make a list of categories of things you'll need to find a home for in your garage. You can always add to it as you go. This list will serve as a basis for determin-ing where each category of items will be located in your garage.

5. Purge.

Before facing an organizing task as overwhelming as a garage, a quick refresher course is in order. Purging is the act of getting rid of things that you no longer need, have a use for, or derive value from. In all the years I've worked with clients, I've yet to work with a client who didn't let go of things during this process. Keep in mind that the organizing process is about making the tough decisions about what to let go of, and then organizing what's left.

Since most people are attached to their things, letting go is often one of the more difficult and emotional steps in organizing. Here are a few tips to help guide you through this process. Ask yourself these questions:

➧ When was the last time I used this item?

➧ Will I realistically ever use it again?

➧ What value does it bring to me?

➧ Could someone else get more use from it than I?

➧ Will I really go out to my garage and dig through a box to get this item and use it?

➧ Will I remember that I've stored it in my garage for future use, or will I end up purchasing a new one because I can't locate it?

◆ Is it really in good enough shape to merit keeping? MaryPat found some treasured books that had suffered mold damage. Clearly, they weren't salvageable, so despite their status as "beloved books," they went in the trash—heartbreaking as it was.

Many times when I work with clients, I hear lots of different reasons and justifications as to why people are hanging on to things. Some common ones are listed below, along with my responses.

"But I might need it someday." It's true, you may need it someday; on the other hand, someday may never come, especially if you've had this item for three years and haven't used it.

"It cost me a lot of money." I understand it cost you a lot of money, but what is it costing you to store the item now? Consider cost in two ways: the money it costs to store things as well as the space you give up for other things. This rationale applied to MaryPat's books and to the children's baby toys.

"My mom, dad, daughter, grandma, [you fill in the blank] gave that to me— how could I part with it?" Each of us can hold on to only so much memorabilia. What are the true treasures that you simply couldn't live without? Do you have a way to display them so you can view them, or are they going to be kept in a box? Consider allowing yourself a certain amount of space to store these types of items and, when that designated space becomes full, taking another look at what you're holding on to.

At the Chengs' garage, every family member got to participate in the purging process. I'd have to say that some family members got the "urge to purge" more than others. To illustrate that this stage can be fun, here are some specific examples of what happened at the Cheng home:

Aaron was given the task of editing his collection of toys, and MaryPat offered him an additional incentive: a small amount of money for each toy he donated. He eliminated more than half of what he originally had, so I'm guessing that he earned enough cash to purchase something new for himself, as well as benefiting many other children from his donations. In order to do this exercise, Aaron was given his existing boxes of toys and asked to consolidate what he was keeping into a bin about half the size of one of the larger bins (photo 4). The other toys went into the donation box.

Catherine was given several boxes of old clothing to sort through. She found a pink sweatshirt jumper decorated with puff paints, sequins, and the like. She also found two Halloween costumes that belonged to her sister, Madeline: a Humpty-Dumpty costume and a butterfly with detachable wings, both sewn by MaryPat. There were lots of giggles as memories were relived, and MaryPat couldn't resist snapping a couple of photos while Catherine held up the outfits.

Madeline, the ballerina in the family, found boxes of old pointe shoes—many of them signed by other ballerinas (photo 6). She spent some time reminiscing about ballets she had performed in, as well as how she had acquired some of the shoes from other ballerinas. In the end, Madeline condensed about 100 pairs down to 10. Most of the shoes Madeline kept were signed by Pacific Northwest Ballet company members or were part of costumes she had worn in *The Nutcracker*, *A Midsummer Night's Dream*, and so on. The shoes Madeline are keeping were to be mounted in a shadow box, so that she'll be able to enjoy seeing them every day instead of having them stuffed in a box in the garage.

MaryPat won the prize for purging the most, and she also lent a little mystery to the proceedings. At one point I heard a loud outburst from her after she found a letter that had been written to her many years back. Aaron and Catherine wanted to know what it was, but MaryPat quickly shoved it in her pocket. My guess is that it was an old love letter!

Tony won the prize for the most agonizing item found (photo 8). As he was sorting through a box of old papers that had been removed from his office and tossed into the garage quite some time ago, he found a check from a client, dated January 26, 2000, in the amount of $3,292.14 (photo 7). The sad thing was that the company that issued the check had since gone bankrupt, so the check couldn't be reissued. Therefore, Tony was out $3,292.14. This is just one of the countless instances in which people have lost money due to clutter and disorganization. Don't let this happen to you!

All in all, each family member had the opportunity to sort and purge many of their belongings on the first day we worked together. At the end of the day, there were still many boxes of items that either belonged in the house or needed to be sorted. As you'll remember, the Chengs had just moved into their house prior to organizing their garage, which is why we found many items in the garage that really did belong in their home. You may not find this to be true in your garage, since each situation is different.

TIP

Remove any items from your garage that you're no longer keeping. If you have time immediately, you can deliver them to donation locations or the dump. If not, choose a deadline by which you'll have these items removed from your home. If you plan to have a garage sale, schedule it on your calendar and make sure you have it on that day—and then donate what's left over.

The Chengs took much more time, without me present, to sort and purge their memorabilia: photos, old schoolwork, home-schooling materials, and letters, to name just a few of the items they discovered. Most people have these types of memorabilia somewhere in their homes, and I always save them for last. Not only are they the most time-consuming items to go through, but there's often more of them, in terms of number of pieces to look at and make decisions on, than other larger items. Just think how many photos can be packed into one large moving box! During the Cheng project, we decided to move all of the boxes of photos, letters, and old school items into their mud room and leave them there as a constant reminder that they needed to be gone through.

MaryPat had eight boxes of memorabilia to go through in about a month's time before I would return to wrap up their garage project. She decided to work on one box at a time so that it would not feel so overwhelming, and she did it in the evenings while watching TV. That way she could even get the kids involved to help her select the favorite family photos to store. They agreed to store their memorabilia in acid-free storage containers, instead of old cardboard boxes and plastic bins, which would not adequately preserve their special memories. For more information on how to organize and store photos and memorabilia, see chapter 12.

6. Group like items together.

Grouping like items together is another critical step in any organizing project. You want to know how much stuff you have in each particular category so that you can proceed with the next two steps, examining the space and shopping.

Since most people are "space-challenged" in their homes, it's important to see exactly what you have that you'll be storing in your garage, so that you can determine the best use of your space. You want to be able to shop according to the space you have and the things you need to organize.

During the sorting phase (step 4), we began our initial grouping of like items. Do not feel as though you need to empty your garage just to get it cleared out, and then wait till later to group like items. You can save yourself a lot of time by establishing categories, as we did, and then refining them during this phase. As mentioned earlier, we uncovered many items in the Chengs' garage that could fit into several of the categories that we established.

This is your final opportunity, now that you've sorted through everything, to really determine how much you have in each category that you'll be storing in your garage. In our project, we didn't finish sorting through everything on the day we began the project; this is normal. Remember, organizing is a process, not an event. These projects take time. The important thing is to keep the process moving toward your final goal.

By the end of this phase, the Chengs' belongings had been sorted, with the exception of the eight boxes of memorabilia. We were now able to see how much we had in each category and make some decisions about how the space would be used in their garage (photo 9).

7. Examine your space.

When you examine your space, you'll need to consider again the purpose you want your garage to serve. In the Cheng garage, we had several goals:

➤ Both cars needed to park in the garage.

◆ A refrigerator and a freezer (two separate units) needed to be in the garage, with quick and easy access from the door connecting the house to the garage.

◆ Both of the large rolling recycling and trash bins needed to have a location with quick and easy access to the door connecting the house to the garage.

◆ The folding Ping-Pong table on wheels needed a home that was easily accessible, so that it could be rolled out and used by the children when the cars weren't parked in the garage.

We also reached a number of other decisions:

◆ We agreed to use the existing workbench area, which had drawers that ran lengthwise along the left wall of the garage, rather than rip it out and install something new in the space.

◆ We agreed that the existing wooden shelves along the back wall would remain in place for storage; however, a couple of them would come down in order to make room for the trash and recycling bins.

◆ We decided to install Onrax hanging storage to handle the sizable quantity of Christmas and other seasonal decorations. In photos 11 and 12, it's hanging from the ceiling, above where the cars park.

◆ MaryPat decided she would like to store all of her gardening-related supplies in the shed in their backyard rather than in the garage.

◆ We decided that the sporting equipment needed to be placed along the back wall of the garage, next to the door that opens to the backyard (photo 12). This would provide quick and easy access to equipment for the kids.

◆ Tony, MaryPat, and I agreed that we could use the rafters in the garage to store items such as folding card tables and chairs, extra carpeting for the house, the window screens, extra pieces of wood trim that may be needed to replace existing trim in the house, and extra shelving for the house.

➤ The existing wood shelves that ran lengthwise on the right side of the garage were only about 6 inches deep, which didn't make good use of the space. We decided to pull them down and instead install two shelving units that were 7 feet high, 8 feet wide, and 30 inches deep to provide optimum storage for all of the remaining bins and luggage (photos 10, 11, and 12).

It was quite easy for us to determine how to use the space after we knew our objectives and could see how much stuff we had to store. The biggest challenges were the refrigerator, freezer, recycling and trash bins, and Ping-Pong table. We needed a location where there was electricity for the refrigerator and freezer, and the doors to both could open with cars parked in the garage. We tried out three different places before we finally settled on a location for these.

> **TIP**
>
> Using the list of categories you created in step 4, draw a quick sketch of where you would like everything to be stored.

After that, things started to fall into place much more easily. We put the trash and recycling bins in front of where the minivan would park (photo 12). Before we got too excited and moved on to the next item, we pulled the minivan into the garage to make sure it would fit. It did! We were in luck.

Now we just had to figure out what to do with the folding Ping-Pong table. It ended up fitting perfectly at the front of the garage, at the end of where we would install the new shelving units.

Here are a few things you may want to consider as you examine the space in your garage:

➤ What purpose do you want your garage to serve?

➤ Do you have space overhead that you can use?

- ◆ If you plan to park your car(s) in the garage and also have storage or other items on either side of the cars, make sure you can get your car doors open.

- ◆ What are the items that you use most often and need easy and quick access to? You'll want to place them near the front of your garage.

- ◆ Keep in mind that neatly stored items take up much less space.

8. Shop!

Now that you've examined your space and know exactly what you have to store, you can shop for products that will help you put the finishing touches on your project as well as products that will store certain items. If you've followed our process and not shopped until now, you will likely be very surprised to discover that you'll need fewer products than you originally imagined. I know this was certainly the case for the Chengs.

9. Install products.

You've sorted, purged, and shopped! Now it's time to install all of the fun new products in your garage that you'll be using to help eliminate the clutter. Installing products can be as simple as putting a new drawer organizer in a drawer, or setting a sports equipment rack on the floor and putting the sports equipment in it. It won't always be necessary to install shelving or hanging storage.

In the Chengs' garage, we did a little bit of each. We had our vendors, Onrax and Empire Shelving, install their storage and shelving units first (photo 10). Then we placed all of our plastic bins and luggage on the storage and shelving units (photos 10 and 11). As mentioned earlier, we'd decided to use the hanging Onrax storage for the holiday decorations (photo 11). This made it very easy to grab all of our bins and place them overhead. Prior to filling them, we labeled each container. Although most of our bins were clear, so you could see through them, labeling eliminated any guesswork as to what was in the bin.

BEFORE YOU SHOP

Prior to going shopping, be sure to do the following:

▶ Make a list of what you're looking for so that you don't forget something. Having a brand in mind will make it easier to get help from salespeople. For example, when MaryPat asked for paint containers, the clerk showed her a painting bucket, but when she told him the containers she wanted were by Rubbermaid, he knew exactly what she was looking for.

▶ Take measurements of wall space, drawers, and so on, and take your tape measure with you so you can measure products at the store.

▶ Make a sketch of your space or a to-scale drawing that you can show to salespeople. A photo of the space can also be useful. If you have a digital camera and can print out a photo on 8½-by-11-inch paper, that will also help a salesperson suggest items that are appropriate for your space.

▶ When you see a picture of a product you like in a catalog, magazine, or newspaper, rip it out and put it in an "ideas" file that you can take with you when shopping.

▶ Be sure to take any coupons that are applicable to your project.

▶ If working on a large project, purchase an expandable file at your local office supply store. In it, you can store your sketches, drawings, photos, clippings, coupons, and any receipts you get from purchases. This will help keep together all of your documentation for the project so that you can find it easily, which will be especially important if any products don't work out and you need to return them.

PRODUCT LIST

STORE	ITEM/SERVICE	SIZE	COST	TOTAL $
Onrax	SL4 overhead storage rack	4' × 8'		249.00
	Installation			119.00
			total	368.00
Empire Shelving	Shelves	8' w × 30" D × 7' H	2 × 241.00	482.00
	Installation		2 × 20.00	40.00
			total	522.00
Other Stores	Drawer organizers and dividers for workbench drawers			8.00
	Freestanding sports equipment organizer			30.00
	Acid-free tubes for artwork and architectural plans			10.00
	Rubbermaid containers for small amounts of paint			26.00
	Various sizes of plastic bins for storage			200.00
			total	274.00
			TOTAL COST OF GARAGE PRODUCTS	**$1,164.00**

The Onrax storage holds up to 500 pounds in the size we installed, so we were able to store a lot of bins on the unit.

Our two shelving units were able to hold most of our plastic bins and all of the luggage. We placed the luggage on the top shelf with the handles facing out, so it would be easy to grab the luggage and go (photo 11). Luggage was a good choice for the top shelf because it's lightweight and easy to lift over the head. We stored extra duffel bags inside some of the luggage to conserve space.

We grouped the bins together in sections on shelves so that they could be quickly located. We divided them into the following categories: toys for nieces and nephews to play with when they visit, keepsake toys, memorabilia, craft supplies, and packing supplies.

We installed the following products on our own:

Sports equipment rack: MaryPat put together the rack, and we filled it with the various equipment and placed it at the back of the garage. It's near the door, so it will be easy for the kids to come in and get what they need, and also easy for them to put equipment away when they're done with it (photo 12)!

Drawer dividers: These were placed in the drawers to hold various supplies and tools. Because the drawers were large, we used shoebox-size plastic boxes as drawer dividers to hold like items together, such as the drill and all of the drill bits and accessories.

Acid-free tubes: We filled these tubes with the Chengs' architectural drawings and the kids' oversized artwork, so they would be protected and wouldn't get wrinkled or destroyed while lying around in the garage.

Paint containers: These Rubbermaid airtight containers, which come in two sizes, were used to store excess paint. We labeled them to indicate which room in the house the paint had been used for. Because we placed them on a shelf above the workbench and close to the door connecting the house to the garage, they're easy to access for quick painting touch-ups.

Now that the products had been installed, we could move the final two items into the garage—the cars! This was an exciting moment for MaryPat and Tony. During their 18 years of marriage, they had never parked their cars in their garage because it had been used for storage. Now, in their new home, they had decided that one of their goals was to be able to park their cars in the garage every day, and we had accomplished it! There were a couple of high fives after the cars were pulled into the garage, and many smiles of happiness with the way the garage had turned out.

10. Maintain.

Although the garage was now organized, that didn't mean we were completely done with the project. As with any organizing project, regular maintenance was still required. Maintenance should be done on an ongoing basis, whether it's in your garage or in another room of the home. Just as if you were to go on a diet and lose weight, you must work at it every day to keep the weight off. Organizing is no different—you must work at maintaining your systems every day to keep the clutter away.

I'm pleased to report that the Chengs' garage is still organized. While MaryPat stated that their garage isn't always neat and tidy, it is organized, and she can find everything! Occasionally she will have a pile of collapsed cardboard boxes waiting to go to recycling or a stash of bags and boxes waiting to be dropped off at a donation location. The key to making sure these items don't pile up over time is for MaryPat to eliminate them as soon as possible. She said there may be tools that haven't yet found their way back to the drawer in the workbench, but since they do have a home, she knows exactly where they should go, and they just need to be put there. This is what it means to maintain.

Now, when MaryPat buys a new item, she thinks about how to store it so she can find and use it. She indicated that she's thinking this way about the new Easter decorations she's getting ready to purchase: she's considering how they'll eventually be stored in the garage when Easter is over.

GARAGE ORGANIZING TIPS

1. Eliminate empty boxes. They are one of the biggest space wasters in a garage or any area of the home. Are you hanging on to boxes because you might ship something in them someday, return a product in them someday, give a gift in them someday, need to put the TV, stereo, or computer in them to move it someday, or all of the above?

Chances are you're storing way too many boxes, and if you break them down, you can regain some valuable space. A few may be important to keep, such as a computer box without which the manufacturer won't take back the product. In most instances, however, if you've had your TV, stereo, or other appliance for more than a year, it's time to let it go. You can always get another box!

If you're hanging onto boxes because you ship lots of gifts around the holidays, remember that if the boxes remain in your garage for any length of time, they'll likely become dusty and musty smelling. Would you really ship something in a box like that? I think not!

The most important part of a box is the product information on the side, which you may want to cut off and store in a filing system instead. That way, if you need to return something, you have the product information at hand.

The Chengs had a number of boxes in their garage that they ended up flattening and recycling (photo 1). They had also kept their moving boxes with the hope of passing them on to someone else or selling them. The low profit margin on selling them (given the time commitment and the price they could reasonably expect) convinced them to list the boxes on Freecycle (www.free cycle.org), an online service where people can post things they want to give away. Most were snapped up by grateful souls. The Chengs had trouble parting with the remaining boxes at first because of the money they'd spent on them, but they finally agreed to recycle them because the cost of not being able to use the garage of their new house was much higher than that of the boxes. Besides, in wet Seattle, the boxes were beginning to get musty and smelly.

2. Look up. Everything in your garage doesn't need to consume valuable floor space. Garages have a lot of overhead wasted storage opportunities. I encourage you to go into your garage, look up, and see how much empty space you have that you could use. Several different products can be used to create additional hanging storage from the beams in your garage; see photos 11 and 12, which show how we were able to incorporate Onrax hanging storage, for instance, into the Chengs' garage.

3. Enlist the help of a friend, if organizing the garage is more than you can bear on your own. You may share a lot of laughs over what you uncover along the way. If you have young children that require your attention, consider having someone watch them while you work so you can stay focused—and, of course, so the kids won't "unsort" everything!

The garage is typically the most underutilized area of the home. What does your garage look like? How would you like it to look? Hopefully you've been inspired by the Cheng family story and are ready to tackle your own garage. I was surprised to learn that we spent just 51 hours organizing their garage, from beginning to end. You too may be surprised at how much you can accomplish in your own garage in just a few short hours.

Good luck!

CHAPTER 10

DOWNSIZING

Downsizing—it's not just for the elderly anymore. Photographs, children's artwork, letters from family and friends, wedding gifts, holiday cards, birthday cards, your child's first outfit: What do all of these items have in common? Most of us have at least some of these life treasures, and often they take up quite a bit of space in our homes.

When you hear the word "downsizing," do you think it doesn't apply to you because you're not old enough to downsize yet? Whatever your age, there will likely come a time when you'll decide that you need or want less. And under the best circumstances, you'll make this choice, rather than having the choice made for you. There are many reasons to downsize at every age. Here are a few:

- You're moving to a smaller space.

- You want to live a more peaceful and simple life.

- You're tired of the burden of maintaining your possessions.

- Your children have left home.

Before taking you through the downsizing process itself, I'd like to share with you a wonderful story about an older client whom we worked with on downsizing.

Margery is 82, and her son Lawson made the arrangements for me to work with her for several days. He had two specific goals in mind:

- To reorganize Margery's kitchen so that she would no longer need to bend over to access things she needed daily.

- To streamline Margery's office so that she would not need to spend most of her day dealing with paperwork, paying bills, and balancing accounts.

When I arrived at Margery's home, she told me several times that she didn't know what we were going to do for so many days. She thought all she needed to do was get a couple of new containers for the flour and sugar. After we had spent 12 hours in her kitchen, eliminating eight boxes of items that were no longer needed, and spent $300 on organizing supplies, Margery's kitchen was more than she had ever envisioned.

The process was rewarding for Margery in several other ways, too. She had the opportunity to take numerous trips down memory lane. We came across all sorts of items that she no longer had a use for, so she was able to pass along these "treasures" to her sons. And we found some wedding gifts she had received more than 50 years ago!

Thus, what began as a project to reorganize Margery's kitchen ended up as an exercise in downsizing. Margery realized that she no longer needed many of her gadgets, extra pots and pans, bakeware, and utensils. We separated the items she no longer had a use for into five categories: items to pass along to each of her two sons, items for her niece, items her housekeeper might want, donations for the church kitchen, and garbage.

As each item was removed from the cupboards or drawers, we determined whether it was used and, if so, how often. If it was no longer needed, we decided which of the five categories it fit in. Along the way, Margery told me the stories of many of her treasures. After going through each cupboard and drawer, we looked at what Margery was keeping and determined the best places for those items. When we were done, we had a kitchen that enabled Margery to reach what she needed daily without bending.

What I discovered through this process is that this project wasn't just about reorganizing Margery's kitchen. It was about guiding Margery in starting to downsize and take a close look at treasures that she was now ready to pass along and share with her family.

Lawson and his brother, Michael, gave their mom an amazing gift: an opportunity for her to start the downsizing process with the assistance of a non–family member. Because I had no emotional attachment to the belongings, I was able to guide Margery through this process, making it easier for all of them. Many times when families undertake this type of activity, there are too many emotions involved, which can lead to fights and misunderstandings. It helps to have a non–family member play the role of facilitator.

After completing this process in the kitchen, we were able to move on to Margery's office and do the same with her paper files. We found many letters and photos. One of Margery's action items after I left was to sort them into the following categories: photos and memorabilia to pass along to Lawson and Michael, photos and memorabilia to keep, photos and memorabilia to pass on to friends, and garbage.

I had Margery do this task on her own because sorting through personal mementos is time-consuming and didn't require my presence. The important point is that Margery now had a system to handle her paper treasures. Because this was in place, she could now tackle a little bit of sorting each day, making the project much more manageable.

During the few days I spent with Margery, she commented several times that if something had happened to her, most of the things she was sorting would have ended up in the garbage rather than being passed on to her loved ones, as she wanted, or donated to a cause she supported. This is very true, and I've seen it happen on a number of occasions.

ASKING THE HARD QUESTIONS

Do you find it difficult to consider downsizing? If so, the following questions may help shed some light on the reasons for your feelings:

- Why are you afraid to let go of these items?
- Are you hanging on to them "just in case"?
- What do these items represent to you?
- How have your treasures and "stuff" affected your family?
- How long are you going to carry things around with you?
- Who said you had to hang on to these things?

You may also want to consider the costs of your present situation.

◆ How much stress are you adding to your life to keep up with all of your possessions?

◆ How much does it cost you to insure all of them?

◆ Do you worry about theft?

◆ How are you going to store them all?

◆ How are you going to clean them all?

THE PROCESS

Just as with any organizing project, sorting and purging are the most time-consuming and daunting phases of downsizing. If you need a quick refresher on the sorting and purging process, see chapter 2. And as with any downsizing project, think of it as a process, something you'll work on for a period of time—as long as you still have the choice to do so.

1. Dedicate time.

There will never be a good time to do this work, so you must make the time. Schedule it on your calendar; otherwise, it will be too easy to put it off for another day. Be sure to allow yourself plenty of time, because this project will likely need to take place over the course of many days, weeks, or maybe even months. I suggest spending two to three hours at a time on it. But if you don't have that much time, don't let that stop you—every little bit counts, even if it's just a half hour.

Downsizing can be very emotionally draining, so you won't want to do it for long periods of time. Many memories and emotions will be stirred up and relived as you sort through years of your life. Be sure to allow yourself enough time to savor the memories as you begin to downsize.

2. Gather supplies.

See the list on page 6 for the supplies you'll need. Make sure to have more than one garbage bag or can! You'll also need colored stickers if you plan to color-code where different items should go.

3. Establish a staging area.

Your staging area for this project should be a location that can house those items that are being downsized (read "leaving the house"). You may even want to consider having two staging areas. One could be a place where you'll permanently keep boxes to put items in that you'll be downsizing. This way, as you come across something you want to let go of, you can take it to that location immediately and be done with it. The second staging location could be in the area where you're working. If that area is full, you may have to create your staging area in the hallway or another room. The more room you give yourself to work in without tripping over anything, the better.

4. Sort.

As mentioned previously, sorting is one of the more time-consuming (and less pleasant) steps of downsizing, but it's a critical step in any organizing process. Without sorting through everything, you simply won't know what you have.

I recommend beginning your downsizing with the kitchen, as strange as that idea may seem. "But I use it every day," I hear you saying. Trust me on this one: you don't use everything in your kitchen every day. The kitchen serves as a great example for downsizing, because everyone has one, and you can apply the process you learn in this room to the other areas of your home.

A kitchen consists of many sections—cupboards, shelves, drawers, and maybe even a pantry—thus making it easy to divide the space into bite-size, manageable pieces. You can ease into this process by starting with one drawer at a time. It's really that simple: just open the drawer and take everything out. (It isn't possible to sort things while they're still in the drawer—I call that shuffling, not sorting.) By emptying the contents of the drawer, you get the opportunity to see everything in there, and I mean everything—including all of the crumbs that have gathered, which I know you'll clean out and wipe down before putting things away.

Organizing is not about shuffling—it is about making decisions and following through with them.

Let's say that you open the utensil drawer that has all of your "very useful" gadgets in it—most of which you may never use. Emptying it out will give you the opportunity to see that you have six wooden spoons, half of which may be broken or stained, and eight spatulas, most of which have melted. When you group like items together (see step 6), you'll begin to see how many like items you have. There's likely not enough space in the drawer to spread everything out so you can really see what you have, which is why it's important to remove the contents of the drawer first.

As you go through the contents of the drawer, you're sure to find items that you no longer use, which can either be donated, given to a family member or friend, or thrown away. Since you already have your boxes set up for donations, and a garbage bag or can handy, it will be a snap to put those items into the appropriate areas. You can then put what's left back into the drawer and move on to the next drawer or cupboard. One drawer should take you no more than 10 to 15 minutes. At that pace, even if you have only one hour to work on this project, you could realistically complete four or five drawers!

If you find that you can't make a decision on a particular item, just set it aside, or put it in another box labeled "Decisions Needed," and move on to the next item. Don't waste your time getting hung up on one item—you can always come back to it later. Remember, you can change your mind on any treasure as long as it's still in your possession. Happily, you most likely won't run into large numbers of sentimental items in the kitchen. Because of this, the decisions you make here will be easier than in other areas of your home. This is another reason why your kitchen may be a great place to start downsizing.

Let's look at another example of sorting: the home office, which often contains several filing cabinets as well as desk drawers and other paper-storage containers, all of which need to be gone through. Unfortunately, a drawer full of papers is going to take you much longer to sort than a drawer in your kitchen. You can pack a lot more paper into a filing drawer than you can pack utensils into a kitchen drawer. A four-drawer filing cabinet can hold 18,000 sheets of paper. Ouch! That's a lot of paper.

Since paper is one of the most time-consuming things to sort, downsizing your office drawers will take you a lot longer than 15 minutes each. You might also have files of paper, letters, cards, and other mementos. In this case, you'll want to allow more time to read those letters and cards. Allow yourself the time to recall the memories, shed some tears, and share the stories. When you're done reading, you can decide whether to "round-file" (read "recycle") the cards and letters or, if you like, pass them on to a family member instead. If you choose to pass them on, be sure to set up a box or envelope for each person to whom you're giving items.

5. Purge.

It's quite possible that you were letting go of things as you were going through the kitchen drawers and cupboards. Do the same in your office: let go of anything that doesn't touch you. Resist the urge to use the excuse that "everything touches me." Instead, think about keeping only those items that remind you of loving relationships, accomplishments in your life, and memorable personal occasions. All of these treasures most likely remind you of the best times in your life.

Since life is not always a bowl of cherries, there may also be items that remind you of sad times, such as mementos of deceased loved ones or major personal transitions. Although these items may stir up bittersweet memories, some may still be worth holding on to or, better yet, passing on to other family members.

Some of the mementos you may want to purge include birthday and holiday cards that have little or no meaning anymore. Many people have volumes of these because they think they'll go back and look at them, yet in reality, rarely does this happen. It's OK to keep cards that contain a personal note with a special meaning to you, but these are likely a small fraction of the total; the rest can be discarded.

Letters are another type of memento people tend to hang on to. Wouldn't it be wonderful to make the time to reread these precious letters you've kept, and then make the decision to pass them on to a family member or friend, or let them go? Take the time now to relive all of these precious memories, and then save only those items that have the most meaning to you.

As you begin the purging process, think about how much space you realistically have to keep letters, cards, and photos. Designate a certain amount of space and allow yourself to save only that amount, or slightly less so that you'll have room to add to it.

6. Group like items together.

Grouping like items means, for instance, grouping all of your birthday cards together, or grouping all of your holiday cards together. You may even want to go one step further and group together birthday cards received in each year, putting a rubber band around them and using a sticky note to label the year. You could do the same for the holiday cards you keep. As an alternative, if you have a few special people from whom you receive cards and letters, you may want to group them by the person who sent them.

7. Examine your space.

As I mentioned at the beginning of this chapter, there are many reasons to downsize. If your reason is that you want to live a more simple life, or that you're tired of maintaining all of your possessions, then space may not be an issue. But if your goal is to move into a smaller space, then you'll definitely need to examine your new space, including all of the closets and any other storage areas, and determine how much you can realistically fit in it. Then look at the items you're keeping, and see if you're on the right track.

Let's use a clothes closet as an example. Keep in mind that most people wear 20 percent of their clothes 80 percent of the time, so you're probably holding on to many pieces of clothing that you haven't worn in a very long time.

Measure the amount of space in feet that your current amount of clothing consumes. Do you have this same amount of feet to hang clothing in your new location? If not, then you may need to return to step 5—purging. Alternatively, you may be able to divide your clothes up differently in your new location. For example, you might divide your clothes by season and store them in two closets instead of one, or store some under the bed.

Remember to be realistic: you can't move 4,000 square feet of possessions into 1,000 square feet, no matter how organized you are! It just doesn't work.

8. Shop!

Congratulations, you've now made it to the most fun part of downsizing—shopping! Now that you've sorted through your cupboards, drawers, closets, and mementos, you should have a very good idea of what you'll need to store and organize. You can now go shopping with a purpose. Be sure to make a list of the items you're looking for, and don't forget to take measurements. This will save you time, because you won't purchase something that won't fit in the space you have. Here are a few examples to illustrate this point.

You've gone through your utensil drawer and now know exactly what you're keeping. If you're moving to a new location, the drawer sizes and configurations may be different. Measure the drawers so you can purchase a drawer organizer that best fills the space and will enable you to see everything. For additional tips on organizing your kitchen, see chapter 4.

You've pared down the number of special cards and letters you're keeping, but you need a way to store these items. Something as simple as a beautiful box with a lid is a great option. These keepsake boxes come in many different sizes, shapes, textures, and colors. Now that you know how much you're keeping, you can shop with a purpose. Perhaps you want one box for cards and letters and another for other types of memorabilia. For additional tips on organizing memorabilia, see chapter 12.

You've survived the agonizing chore of downsizing your clothes and are now seeking a clever way to make sure what you're keeping will fit into the space. This may begin with analyzing the layout of the closet and determining whether you're maximizing the space. Perhaps you need to purchase some hangers that will allow you to hold five pairs of pants or skirts on one hanger, or five shirts on one hanger. Maybe you need containers that fit under your bed to hold off-season clothing, or a moveable wardrobe that you can store in another area to hold the clothes that don't fit into the existing closet. Or the solution may be to reconfigure the closet entirely. You might choose to do this on your own, with a closet organizing kit or product available from do-it-yourself stores, or have a custom closet installed. For additional ideas on closet organizing, see chapter 5.

9. Install products.

Depending on the type of products you purchase, the installation may take just a few minutes and be a snap, or it could take you several hours. Using our examples in this chapter, if you've purchased drawer organizers, it should take you just a few minutes to put the organizer in the drawer and arrange the drawer's contents in it. The same applies to any type of boxes you purchase to store memorabilia. In your closet, if you've chosen to install a new organizing system, that will be much more time consuming—but so worth it!

10. Maintain.

Maintenance is the key to any organizing project. Maintenance is the little things you do on a regular basis to maintain the new systems that you've worked hard to establish. Without regular maintenance, the time you've invested in your organizing project will have been wasted.

Let's demonstrate by using two of our previous examples from this chapter, clothes and memorabilia.

Clothes: If you're like me, you love to shop for clothes! The problem is, you have only so much space. It's easy to shop and bring home more clothes, but how often do you think about letting go of items you no longer wear because they don't fit, are outdated, are damaged, or just don't make you feel good anymore? Make an agreement with yourself that whenever you purchase new clothes, you'll remove the same number of items from your closet. No, this doesn't mean just moving them to a different closet—it means letting go, because you know you aren't going to wear them anyway. If you practice this regularly after you've downsized your closet, your closet will never overflow.

Memorabilia: You've already designated a location and a specific amount of space for memorabilia. Now all you need to do is place these special items in the designated location. When the area that you designated becomes full, it's time to do a bit of purging—so that new items will fit!

Now that you've gone through all of the hard work of deciding what to downsize, there's one final step you must complete: making sure those items get moved from your home to their new location. Examples of this step may include taking out the trash, dropping items off at donation locations, and contacting your friends and family to pick up items you've earmarked for them. Be sure to follow through and complete the task, or you'll still be burdened.

DOWNSIZING TIPS

When you've decided you're ready to start downsizing, here are some tips to help.

1. Begin in the areas you're not currently using, such as extra bedrooms, the basement, the attic, or the garage. This will be less disruptive to your daily life, and these areas are likely to contain items that haven't been used in a long time and won't be missed when passed on.

2. Set up boxes to put things in for donations, to sell, to toss, or to give to your children or friends. Label each box so you know which is which. Sort directly into the appropriate box so that you don't have to re-sort these items later. This will save you time.

3. Color-code your possessions. Affixing different-colored stickers to items that you will keep, toss, donate, give to someone, or sell (at a garage sale, consignment store, or auction).

4. Tackle big items first, such as furniture. Use sticky notes to label the furniture, or keep a list of which items go to who. You'll see results more quickly when you start with the big items first. If you start with the smaller stuff, the task may seem overwhelming and you may give up before you really get started.

5. Eliminate items that no longer have value to you or bring you joy.

6. Enlist the help of a friend. Perhaps you can find someone who's also interested in going through this process, and take turns helping each other. It's more fun to do this work with a buddy.

7. Focus. Resist the urge to do a little here and a little there. You'll feel as though you haven't accomplished a thing. Tackle one room, one closet, or one drawer at a time until it's done, and then move on.

8. Assign your belongings. Make a list of the treasures you're ready to part with now. Assign names to each one—perhaps people who have admired a specific item, or people you would like to see have a particular item. You could write a brief story about the item and then share that story as you pass along your gift.

9. Save only what you have space for.

10. Don't force "overstock" into everyday areas. Establish a location for these items.

11. Sort items into two categories, active and archive. Store archive items in less accessible locations.

12. Look up. Use tall bookshelves or shelves mounted on the wall.

13. Use bed risers so you can store items under the beds.

14. Where possible, double-hang clothes in the closet.

15. Make full use of cabinets with turntables, stair-stepped risers, or pull-out drawers.

16. Use the backs of doors to store shoes, hats, towels, and pantry items.

17. Try to store your treasures in pieces that have two purposes—such as a coffee table that holds treasures in baskets below, or a trunk that holds treasures and serves as a coffee table as well.

18. Don't think in terms of how much you can fit into the space. Decide which belongings are important. Focus on creating space around these items.

19. Keep your systems simple.

20. Purge regularly!

GRANDMA MARIE'S STORY

After my grandpa passed away at the age of 91, my grandma, aunt, and uncles were the ones who spent time downsizing the very few personal possessions he had. Because Grandma was still alive, most of what was in the house remained. Last year I took Grandma to one of the organizing supply stores I shop at frequently. It just so happened that this store was one of the places where I give organizing seminars, and my upcoming seminar was about downsizing. Grandma saw the event poster in the store and started telling me about how she was starting to downsize.

She said she had gathered boxes for each person in the family: one for each of her three remaining children, one for each of her 10 grandchildren, and one for each of her 11 great-grandchildren. As she came across things she thought each of us might like, she would place them in the appropriate box. She planned to give each of us the contents of our box when we visited her, and let us decide what to do with it. Grandma recognized one important rule of downsizing: "Accept the fact that what you give to others, they may not want."

On my last couple of visits to Grandma's house, I've received a variety of things, including piano music that used to be my mom's, photos, and my birth announcement. Since I must practice what I preach, of those things that Grandma gave me, I kept just a few: some of the photos and my birth announcement. I gave away the duplicate copies of the photos to other family members, and after I had my "moment" with my mom's piano music, I actually threw it out—mostly because it was moldy from being in Grandma's garage all of those years.

Although I was sad at the thought of my grandma starting this process, I was also very proud of her for doing this for all of us. (You're probably thinking that I had something to do with this, but I guarantee you, I did not!) It's a wonderful opportunity for my grandma to go through her treasures while she is alive and then reminisce about the past with her children, grandchildren, and great-grandchildren when she passes those treasures to us. There are many stories that are being told now—a wonderful opportunity for all of us to share.

MOVING FORWARD

The following are a few final thoughts that may help further inspire you to downsize:

1. Downsizing means unburdening yourself from things that tie you to the past. It will free you up to face the future and enjoy life every day.

2. If you postpone the need to lighten the load, you may end up burdening someone else.

3. If your goal is to simplify your life, you don't need to get rid of everything. You may just need to pare down your possessions, keeping only your favorite things, the things that you want to be surrounded by, or those items that you need or enjoy using.

4. What you use in your home on a daily basis probably amounts to a fraction of what you own. Think about it!

Your attitude toward the downsizing process is everything. It can make the difference in assuring the ease and success of your project. Approach downsizing with the end in mind—a simpler, happier, more carefree life—and you'll enjoy it much more. Downsizing is something almost all of us will have to do at some point, so having a system for tackling this project will benefit you greatly.

CHAPTER 11

WHAT TO DO WITH ALL THAT PAPER

S tudies show that about 80 percent of the paper people hold on to is never referenced again. That's a lot of paper. Paper comes into your home every day—from the mail, to papers you bring home from work, to papers your children bring home from school.

This chapter will first help you identify paper that you can discard right away. Next, we'll address how to deal with the mail—a major source of paper inflow to any household. Finally, we'll cover how to store truly valuable papers.

ELIMINATE IT—PAPER YOU SHOULD TOSS

G et out the recycling bin and the shredder! Below are some examples of the many kinds of paper that you can eliminate immediately, before they have a chance to create clutter:

- ◆ Junk mail
- ◆ Receipts for groceries, movie rentals, personal care items, clothes you won't return, meals (if you don't need to deduct them for business reasons), after they have been recorded in your checkbook or computer software
- ◆ Invitations to events you know you won't attend
- ◆ Bad-quality photos or ones you just don't like
- ◆ Receipts for non-tax-deductible items
- ◆ Solicitations from charities you don't intend to give to
- ◆ Newspapers you don't intend to read
- ◆ Envelopes from the daily mail you open
- ◆ Prospectuses from stocks you own that you'll never read
- ◆ ATM receipts (after you've recorded them)
- ◆ Bank deposit slips (after you've recorded them)

- Inserts included with utility bills, credit card statements, and banking statements

The following are some other kinds of papers that can be eliminated after their purpose has been served. If you have any questions about which paperwork you must keep for tax purposes, contact your tax preparer or a certified public accountant.

- Expired coupons
- Newspapers that are more than a week old
- Old greeting cards (unless they contain a very special message)
- Invitations to past events
- Outdated schedules
- Expired warranties and service contracts
- Instructions for items you no longer own
- Expired insurance policies (keep only the declarations page)
- Unread magazines that are more than three months old
- Old catalogs (keep only the current ones)
- Investment and banking brochures you've never read
- Cancelled checks (unless needed for tax purposes)
- Checkbooks that are more than six years old, or for accounts that are closed
- Tourist brochures from past vacations
- Road maps you haven't referred to in five years
- Recipes you haven't tried in a year
- Articles or clippings you haven't reread in more than five years
- Credit card statements that are more than a year old

- Utility bills that have been paid (unless you deduct a home office as a business expense; if so, save these for your taxes)
- Paycheck stubs (after you receive your W-2 statement in January)
- Airline boarding passes that are more than one year old (you won't be able to claim mileage after a year)
- Travel itineraries from completed trips
- Mortgage statements that have been paid (but keep the 1099-INT statement you receive from your lender in January, showing the amount of interest you paid that year, to file with your taxes)

WHAT TO DO WITH ALL THAT MAIL

The U.S. Postal Service delivers 206 billion pieces of mail per year. That's 563 million pieces per day, and more than 6,000 items per second! No wonder we all seem to receive so much mail.

A while back, I did an experiment with my mail. For two weeks I kept every piece of mail I received, including the envelopes, in a pile after I opened it. At the end of the two weeks I had between eight and nine inches of mail, most of which could have been tossed immediately.

I've worked with clients who would rather have a root canal than open their mail. For some reason, they just cannot bring themselves to do it. This poses a big problem when the mail contains bills that need to be paid. Over time, the late fees assessed on unpaid bills can add up to a small fortune, not to mention the effect on your credit score, especially if you miss mortgage payments. I always advise such clients to sign up with an electronic bill-paying service immediately.

I don't know what it is about the mail that people despise so much, but I have a feeling that part of the problem is the lack of a good system for processing mail. Mail should be processed on a daily basis. A good system for processing mail includes a place to put what needs to be kept and a commitment to toss the rest immediately. Without a system it becomes overwhelming, and that's why many simply choose to ignore the mail in hopes that it will vanish into thin air. Here are two steps you can take to better manage your mail:

1. Remove your name from mailing lists.

Every time you provide your name and address when you enter a sweepstakes, fill out a product registration, or make a catalog purchase, your name may be added to a mailing database, which could later be sold. Although you may not be able to eliminate all of the junk mail, you can substantially reduce it. The key is to be persistent.

Unfortunately, there's no one-stop-shopping outlet that can remove your name from all of the mailing lists you're on. Instead, you'll need to contact a number of different companies and organizations. The more frequently used resources are listed below for your convenience.

After you have sent in your requests, keep in mind that it may take anywhere from three to six months before you start to see a decrease in the amount of junk mail you receive. Be patient; it will be worth the wait!

Direct Marketing Association

Asking the Direct Marketing Association's Mail Preference Service (MPS) to take you off their mailing lists is a good first step to reduce the flow of advertising mail from national marketers such as credit cards, sweepstakes and magazine subscription offers, and catalogs. After five years, your request will expire and you'll need to reregister with MPS.

Not all companies use the MPS to purge their mailing lists, unfortunately, so you may continue to receive some promotions. Also, local businesses and organizations usually don't use this program. And you'll continue to receive mail from companies with which you already do business. In these instances, you'll need to contact the companies directly and ask to be placed on their do-not-mail list.

Direct Marketing Association
Mail Preference Service
PO Box 643
Carmel, NY 10512
Online: www.dmaconsumers.org/offmailinglist.html
Phone: (888) 241-6760, 8 a.m. to 5 p.m. EST

Catalog Mailing Lists

The Abacus database consists of names and addresses of people who have made purchases from participating mail-order catalogs. Once your name is added to this database, it could be sold to other companies, which will then send you unsolicited catalogs.

Abacus
PO Box 1478
Broomfield, CO 80038
E-mail: optout@abacus-direct.com

Note: Not all companies participate in the Abacus opt-out program. If you continue to receive some catalogs, you'll need to contact those companies directly.

Preapproved Credit Card Offers

You have three credit reports—one from each of the three following companies. You may wish to have your name removed from these companies' lists so that you no longer receive preapproved credit card offers.

Equifax
Marketing Decision Systems
PO Box 740123
Atlanta, GA 30374-0123
888-567-8688

Experian
Target Marketing Services Division
Attn: Mail Preference Service
PO Box 919
Allen, TX 75013
888-397-3742

TransUnion
Name Removal Option
PO Box 505
Woodlyn, PA 19094-0605
888-567-8688

Sweepstakes

When you register to win a prize or sweepstakes, you're also requesting that your name be added to mailing lists used by other sweepstakes promoters. You can request that your name be removed from these lists by contacting the following companies. The best way to reduce the number of sweepstakes mailings you receive, of course, is to not participate in the first place.

American Family Publishers (does not rent or sell its database)
PO Box 62000
Tampa, FL 33662

Publisher's Clearinghouse (does not rent or sell its database)
101 Channel Drive
Port Washington, NY 11050
Note: Be sure to list each name exactly as it's listed on the envelope.
Phone: 800-645-9242 (8:30 a.m.–8:30 p.m. EST)
Fax: 800-453-0272

Reader's Digest Sweepstakes (does not rent or sell its database)
Readers Digest Road
Pleasantville, NY 10570

Nonprofit Organizations

If you've ever donated money or items to nonprofit organizations, chances are that you're on not only their mailing list, but also the mailing lists of other nonprofit organizations, because these organizations exchange and rent their lists. If you would like to be taken off their lists, you'll need to contact them directly.

America Online (AOL)

To stop receiving discs from America Online, call 800-605-4297 and ask to have your name removed from the mailing list.

ValPak

To stop receiving ValPak mailings, complete the online form at www.coxtarget.com/mailsuppression/s/DisplayMailSuppressionForm.

Missing Children Postcards (ADVO)

ADVO's Have You Seen Me? cards, which feature the names and faces of missing children, reach up to 85 million households each week, are seen by more than 120 million people, and have become the most recognized piece of mail in America.

> **ADVO**
> PO Box 249
> Windsor, CT 06095
> 888-241-6760 (8 a.m.–5 p.m. EST)
> Online: www.advo.com/consumersupport.html

Sexually Oriented Advertising (SOA)

To stop receiving these notices, complete Form 1500, Application for Listing and/or Prohibitory Order, at www.usps.com, or pick one up at your local Post Office.

Other Tips for Reducing Junk Mail

Call your phone company and request that your phone number be unlisted, or at least ask them not to print your mailing address in the phone book. Many mailing lists are created from the white pages.

Be careful which warranty cards you send in for products you purchase. Some companies will use this information to send you advertisements for other products. In most cases you're still covered under the warranty even if you don't send in the card. If you're unsure, send in the card with minimal information, such as only your name and the product's serial number.

Be aware that a major lifestyle change, such as a move, is considered to be a matter of public record and is therefore not considered confidential. Other information that's a matter of public record includes the sale or purchase of a home, a birth, or a marriage. Advertisers get your address from these records and send you coupons or insurance offers for your new home, for example. If you don't wish to receive these types of offers, you'll need to contact each company individually and ask to have your name removed from their database.

Moving and Changing Your Address with the U.S. Postal Service

A side benefit of moving is that your junk mail will subside . . . at least for a while! A month before you move, fill out the Postal Service's "Change of Address Form" (PS Form 3575), and it will forward the following mail to you:

◆ First-class mail, Priority Mail, and Express Mail for 12 months, unless otherwise requested by mailer

◆ Newspapers and magazines for 60 days

◆ Packages weighing 16 ounces or more for 12 months, locally

Note: Circulars, books, catalogs, and advertising mail under 16 ounces won't be forwarded unless requested by the mailer.

Once the Postal Service receives the Change of Address Form, they'll send you a notice confirming the receipt. If you prefer, you can fill out the same form online at www.usps.com. You'll pay a small credit-card fee to complete the transaction. The Post Office charges this fee so they can verify that it is you requesting the address change.

2. Open and process your mail on a daily basis.

The best way to keep the amount of mail and paper clutter to a minimum is to deal with it on a daily basis. This should take no more than five minutes a day. Some mail will require additional action, such as paying a bill or making a phone call. Unless you feel compelled to pay your bills as they arrive, you can put these action items in a location you've designated, and handle them later.

Here are some tips to help you process mail daily:

(a) Establish a place where you will process the mail. Suitable options may include the kitchen counter, the kitchen table, the dining room table, the laundry room, the office, and the den.

(b) If your mail isn't delivered directly to your front door and you have to walk to the mailbox to get it, you can sort it on your walk back. You can do a quick scan and pull out all of the junk by the time you get back to the house. If you have a recycling bin in the garage or outside your home, you can toss the junk mail into the bin before entering your home. If this isn't an option, or you need to shred some of the junk, bring it into your mail processing area. Create a stack of mail that can go directly into the recycling bin and a stack that needs to be shredded.

(c) If you don't have a paper shredder, buy one. The small investment you make could save you countless hours of frustration by preventing identity theft, which could ruin your credit score. Put the shredder near where you will process the mail, thus making it easy for you to place the unwanted mail in the shredder immediately.

In my home, I have two shredders—one in the kitchen, because I open the mail at the kitchen counter, and one in my office upstairs. I process all of my mail at the counter before taking it to my office to be stored. When the shredder is full, I empty it into the recycling bin. (I also place paper to be recycled into the shredder without shredding it, to save me a trip to the recycling bin.) I keep an additional shredder in my office so I don't have to walk downstairs if I need to shred important documents with personal information on them.

(d) Establish areas in your home for the following types of items, which you likely receive in the mail on a regular basis: bills to be paid, papers to be filed, reading materials such as magazines and newspapers, correspondence that needs action, mail for other family members, invitations to parties and events, and coupons.

(e) When establishing where to place mail for other family members, be sure to involve them in the decision. You want to choose a location that they'll remember to check each day, so they don't miss something that needs immediate attention.

I worked with one client, John, whose wife would set his mail on his chair in the office. Although it was hard to miss, he didn't like having to pick it up and move it to another location so he could sit down. Our very simple solution was to place an in-box on his desk that was for incoming mail only. His mail was still always in one place, but he no longer had to move it. And by placing the mail in the in-box on the desk, not directly on the desk, we eliminated the possibility of the mail getting lost on the desk amid all of his other projects.

(f) Make sure that all appropriate family members know where the "bills to be paid" area is located.

(g) If you don't plan to file papers daily that require no action but that you must keep, establish a location for them. Ensure that all family members know that this location is only for papers that require no action. You don't want a family member placing a bill or other important item in an area that you don't look at often.

(h) Eliminate envelopes. You don't need them. I've watched many of our clients open their mail, look at it, and then shove the contents back into the envelope. If you need the envelope because you want to record the address, tear off the address and place it in your address book to be added later, or place it by your computer to enter into an electronic database. Better yet, take a minute now and add it to your address list so that you can then get rid of it entirely.

(i) Establish a location for things that need to be mailed. For example, if you leave every day through the garage, consider hanging a basket or a mail slot on the wall as a gathering place for all outgoing mail. Then you can grab it as you leave the house and not have to worry about it getting lost in the shuffle.

Having read all of these tips on processing mail daily, you should find the following steps very simple to follow:

1. Bring in the mail—each day! Don't let it pile up or it will become overwhelming, and then you won't want to open all of it and sort it out.

2. Sort the mail into two piles: junk and mail to keep.

3. Get rid of the junk—now! Toss it in the recycling bin, or shred it if necessary. Most likely you'll be able to identify the junk without even opening it. You can save yourself time by running the entire contents of the envelope through the shredder if you know you don't need to open it.

4. Open the remaining mail. As you open the mail, set the envelopes aside in a pile. Toss them after all of the mail is opened. Toss any unnecessary inserts that come with your bills or statements. The stack of mail that you have left should now be very small. Some days when I'm done opening all of my mail, I have only one or two items I need to do something with.

5. Place the remaining mail in the locations established in tips (d) and (g) on page 185.

Processing the mail daily doesn't have to be painful. The key is to establish a system that works for you. Use your system each day, and be sure the rest of your family understands it.

BETTER SAFE THAN SORRY: STORING IMPORTANT PAPERS

Many documents in your possession may be either impossible or extremely difficult to replace should the need arise. Often the best solution is to store documents you might need right away in a fireproof box in your home, and to store the rest in a safe deposit box at your bank. Whichever solution you select, be sure to follow through. You or your loved ones will be glad you did.

Items to Store at Home

If you have items you (or someone else) might need immediately in case of emergency, you should keep those at home rather than at a bank. Such items include the following:

➧ Passport (in case you need to take a sudden trip outside the country)

➧ Power of attorney originals

➧ Will

➧ Living will or any medical directive

➧ Funeral or burial instructions (in case they're needed over the weekend)

Other Items to Protect

Here's a list of some other items you may want to protect in a secure environment, either at home or at your bank. This is intended to start you thinking, not to serve as a complete list.

➧ Adoption papers (originals only)

➧ Automobile titles

- Bank account numbers and contact information
- Baptismal and other religious certificates
- Birth certificates (originals only)
- Cemetery deeds (originals only)
- Child custody agreements or parenting plans (originals only)
- Citizenship papers (originals only)
- Collectibles that are valuable
- Credit card account numbers (copy the front and back of each card so you have both the account number and the customer service number)
- Death certificates (originals only)
- Diplomas
- Divorce decrees (originals only)
- Employee benefit records
- Family historical information
- Household inventory and appraisals of antiques, artwork, collectibles, and furs; you may also want to include photos or videos to help document these items
- Immunization records
- Important contracts
- Insurance policy names and numbers—(home or renter's, auto, medical, life)
- Investment certificates
- Jewelry and jewelry appraisals
- Leases
- Marriage certificates (originals only)
- Medals

- Military records
- Mortgages
- Naturalization certificates
- Negatives of important photos, such as those from your wedding
- Patents and copyrights
- Photos of possessions
- Rare stamps and coins
- Real estate deeds
- Retirement plan information
- Stock and bond certificates
- Veterans' papers

In Case of Emergency

You'll also want to determine in advance who will be able to have access to your safe deposit box in case of an emergency. Different states have different laws on who can access the box after your death. Some states make it easy for a family member or the executor of the estate to access the box, while other states require a court order to access it, which would take time and money.

One solution is to rent your safe deposit box jointly with a spouse, child, or someone else. That person would need to sign the rental agreement as well, and would then usually have unrestricted access to the box. In some states, however, there still may be delays before the co-renter of the box could access the contents after your death. Note that simply giving someone a key to your safe deposit box doesn't give them permission to access the box; their name needs to be on the rental agreement as well.

Insuring the Contents of a Safe Deposit Box

Be sure to read the rental agreement for your safe deposit box carefully. Banks don't insure what you put in the box. Fire, floods, and theft are very rare at banks, but they do happen. Most banks will be liable only if you can prove that they were negligent and failed to use reasonable care to prevent a loss. If you're concerned about this, you should check with your insurance agent to find out if you need additional coverage for items placed off-site (such as jewelry, coins, and stamps), over and above your homeowner's or renter's insurance policy. Also note that if you're storing checks or cash in your safe deposit box, these won't be covered by the bank's FDIC insurance, since you haven't deposited them directly into your account.

Creating an Itemized List of Contents

The final step in organizing your important papers and valuable items is to create an itemized list of the possessions you're storing in your safe deposit box, fireproof box, or both. Be sure to list the location of each item and the date it was stored. Periodically, review the contents to see if you need to update any of the items being stored, such as banking or credit card information. If you have a safe deposit box, take the itemized list with you whenever you visit the bank, and update it while you're there.

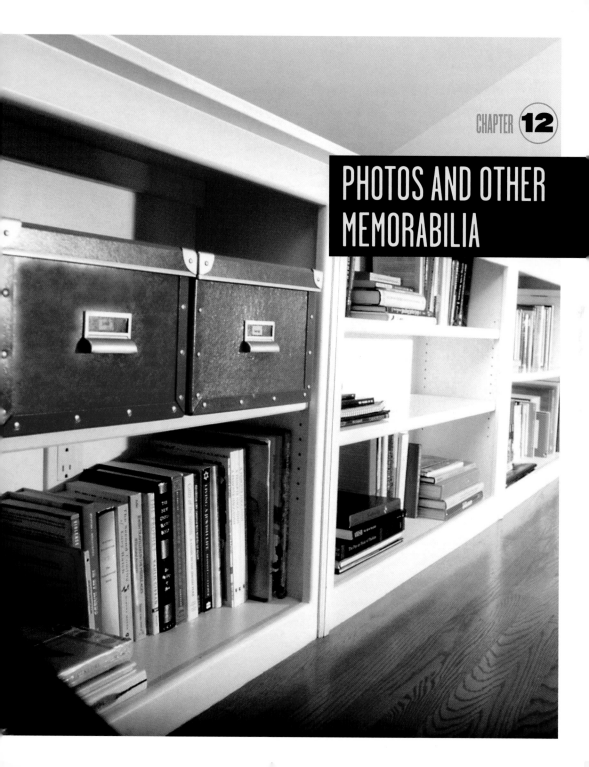

CHAPTER 12

PHOTOS AND OTHER MEMORABILIA

Photos, artwork by your children, a special gift from a parent, the program from your wedding, a college diploma, the wristband from the hospital when your child was born—what do all of these items have in common? They could all be considered memorabilia or keepsake items. Organizing memorabilia can sometimes be a big challenge, especially when there are a lot of items and many different types of keepsakes.

Most of this chapter will be dedicated to organizing photos, both printed and digital; however, I'll also suggest a few ways of organizing non-photo-related memorabilia. To obtain the supplies discussed in the chapter, such as photo boxes, albums, scrapbooks, and CD/DVD storage devices, visit your local office supply, craft supply, or organizing store, or see the "Shopping Resources" appendix for an array of online stores.

ORGANIZING PHOTOS

Until recently, our clients had challenges organizing years' worth of printed photos. Now, with digital photography being so popular, there's a new set of challenges—how to store all of the images taken. I'll discuss several different methods for organizing both print and digital photos.

Printed Photos

Many clients tell me they simply can't think about organizing their printed photos because it's too overwhelming. If you don't have time to organize your printed photos at present, there are three things you can begin doing now that will make the task go faster in the future:

> ◆ When you pick up your newly developed photos, eliminate those that are poor quality, blurred, or trivial; those that you simply don't like; and those that are similar to others. Duplicates, and photos that are similar to others, can be given to others—but do so right away, while they're

still current. Drop them in the mail to a friend or family member with a quick note—it's a great way to brighten someone's day.

◆ At a minimum, write the date (month and year) and the occasion on the envelope. It will take you two seconds—well worth it to eliminate the frustration you'd feel in the future while trying to remember when the photos were taken.

◆ Establish a location where you place photos in their envelopes until you're ready to organize them. This can be as simple as putting them in a photo storage box until you're ready to put them in albums, scrapbooks, or some other system.

Storage

Three of the more popular storage methods are photo boxes, photo albums, and scrapbooks.

For some, the easiest way to store and organize photos is to place them in photo boxes and label them. The drawback of this method is that when someone wants to look at your photos, you may end up with fingerprints on them, plus individual photos take longer to locate.

Putting photos into either photo albums or scrapbooks, on the other hand, provides you with an opportunity to display your photos as well as your creativity, while organizing the photos in a way that will keep fingerprints off them.

It's no secret that photos stored for any length of time should be kept in acid-free storage. Most photo preservationists today believe that photos should be kept in lignin-free storage as well, since lignin is believed to be more harmful to prints than acid.

Lignin is found in the paper and board products used to create some kinds of photo storage boxes and other photo storage media.

Categories

Before you begin organizing your photos, have a plan. Determine the type of storage you want to use, as well as how you would like to organize the photos that go into the type of storage you've selected. Some options are by year, by family member, and by occasion.

You may want to select more than one type of storage and more than one organizing option. For example, let's say you want to organize your photos by family member using photo storage boxes, but you want to capture the special moments from your wedding in a photo album and gather the memories from a family reunion into a scrapbook. As with any organizing project, there's no right or wrong way to organize your photos.

Labeling

When labeling your photos, be sure to use a pen or pencil that's of archival quality, so as to not destroy your photos over the long term.

When labeling multiple copies of the same photo (such as your child's school portrait or a wedding photo) before giving them to others, consider using labels that you print on a computer. You can create a sheet of the same label and place one on the back of each photo. It's a lot faster than labeling each photo by hand, and it looks great.

Storing Negatives

Safely storing negatives of certain once-in-a-lifetime occasions, such as a wedding, the birth of a child, or a 90th birthday celebration, may be just as important as organizing the actual photos. There are many different ways to store your negatives, besides in the sleeves they come in. For example, you can purchase ring binder inserts, polypropylene three-hole sleeves (which can be used in binders or with hanging bars to hang in a filing system), and specially designed acid-free storage boxes for negatives. If your negatives are extremely important, you may want to protect them by storing them in a fireproof box at home or a safe deposit box at your bank (see chapter 11).

Scanning Photos

A number of resources are available on the Web for scanning your photos, slides, and negatives and transferring them to CD or DVD. If you wish to scan a large number of photos but don't have much free time, it may be worth the small investment to pay a service to do the scanning for you.

If you choose to scan your own photos, refer to the discussion of photo-naming conventions later in this chapter, in the section on organizing digital photos.

Avoiding Damage to Photos and Negatives

Heat, humidity, lights, pollutants, framing, and improper handling can all damage photos and negatives. You should also avoid storing them near perfume, solvents, paints, adhesives, or mothballs, as fumes from these products can be harmful. Wear gloves when sorting negatives and slides, because oils in your hands can cause damage.

If you're unsure whether the photo boxes, photo albums, scrapbook pages, photo corners, or other products you're using are acid-free, use a pH test pen to instantly check the levels of acid in these products. You can purchase one through some of the resources listed later in this chapter.

DIGITAL PHOTOS

Organizing digital photos also requires you to create a system so that you can easily locate and retrieve a specific photo when you want to print or e-mail it to someone. Without a good system, you could spend hours searching through all the photos you've downloaded from your digital camera to your computer.

I recommend that you create one location on your computer to store these photos. Below I present two examples of main folders:

- Laura—Pictures (with "—")
- Laura Pictures (without "—")

Think of your main folder as a filing cabinet for photos on your computer. After you create it, you will then create subfiles, which will represent the filing cabinet drawers where the photos will actually be stored. When naming your subfiles, be as specific as possible, including the name of the event or occasion, the person's name, and the date.

In order to explain the file structure I'm suggesting, I've provided two examples, each of which organizes the same collection of photos in different ways. In fact, there's an infinite number of possible arrangements; it all depends on your personal preference.

Example I

File Structure—Collapsed View

In this collapsed view, you can see that I've established eight folders, which hold images relating to Cats, Christmas, Events, Family, House Projects, Laura—Professional, Mozart, and Vacations. When I expand these folders, I see the following.

File Structure—Expanded View

Here's why I've created this file structure:

- Cats: I have a lot of them, so instead of storing all of their photos in one folder called Cats, I created subfiles for each cat. Similarly, if you have children, you could have a folder called Children or Kids and then a subfile for each child.

◆ Christmas: Because I take a lot of photos at Christmas, I like to have a subfile for each year, rather than one big file called Christmas. That way I know what year every photo was taken.

◆ Events: This folder holds photos of different parties or celebrations I've attended. Instead of creating a folder for each type of event from the main folder, Laura—Pictures, I decided to create an Events folder that could be used to hold images of a wide variety of events, with a sub-file for each event.

◆ Family: In this folder I keep special photos of family members. There aren't many photos in the folder now, which is why it has no subfiles. I anticipate needing subfiles for some family members in the future, and all I'll need to do at that time is create a subfile labeled with their name.

◆ House Projects: Not only do I love to help our clients get organized, I also love to do similar projects around my own home. I always take "before" and "after" photos, because it gives me a great feeling of accomplishment to see how I've been able to transform a space. In this example, I've chosen to create subfiles for two of my current projects.

◆ Laura—Professional: Here I keep photos for my marketing materials and Web site. Every few years I have them updated, so I keep a subfile with the date of each.

◆ Mozart: Mozart is my Saint Bernard. Because I have only one dog, I didn't find it necessary to create a folder called Dogs similar to the Cats folder. Instead, Mozart gets his own folder.

◆ Vacations: I love to take vacations, and I take a lot of them. I create a subfile for each vacation and label it with the destination and the date, so that there's no guesswork in the future.

Example 2

File Structure—Collapsed View

This file structure uses the exact same photos as the previous example, but organizes them in a different way. In this example, here's what I did differently:

◆ Animals: Both the Cats and Mozart files comprise this folder.

◆ Family Events: This replaces the Family folder.

◆ Holidays: This is a new folder to which I can add other holidays in the future, not just Christmas.

◆ Professional Work Photos: This folder was formerly Laura - Professional; I simply renamed it but didn't change its structure.

◆ Projects: I've broadened the label of this folder so I can use it to store photos of any projects I work on, house-related or not.

◆ Special Occasions: This folder was named Events in our last example. This is just an example of how you can use different words to reference the same information.

◆ Vacations: I retained the label Vacations for this folder, but I changed the structure of the subfiles and created folders for each year of vacations instead. I did this because I know that there will be many more vacation folders in the future.

File Structure—Expanded View
Here's why I changed the structure of my first example:

◆ Animals: Instead of having two separate folders for my animals, Cats and Mozart, I'm able to have a subfile for each animal or group of animals. This keeps all of my animal photos in one location. It also gives me a place to put the Kittens folder with its subfiles, instead of grouping it with Cats.

◆ Family Events: There are two main events for which I currently have digital photos, so I decided to create a subfile for each event and label it with the event name and date.

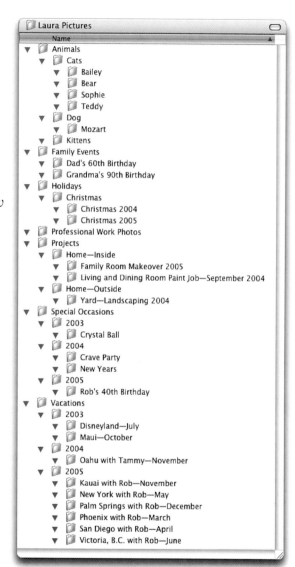

Laura Pictures

Name
▼ 🗀 Animals
　▼ 🗀 Cats
　　▼ 🗀 Bailey
　　▼ 🗀 Bear
　　▼ 🗀 Sophie
　　▼ 🗀 Teddy
　▼ 🗀 Dog
　　▼ 🗀 Mozart
　▼ 🗀 Kittens
▼ 🗀 Family Events
　▼ 🗀 Dad's 60th Birthday
　▼ 🗀 Grandma's 90th Birthday
▼ 🗀 Holidays
　▼ 🗀 Christmas
　　▼ 🗀 Christmas 2004
　　▼ 🗀 Christmas 2005
▼ 🗀 Professional Work Photos
▼ 🗀 Projects
　▼ 🗀 Home—Inside
　　▼ 🗀 Family Room Makeover 2005
　　▼ 🗀 Living and Dining Room Paint Job—September 2004
　▼ 🗀 Home—Outside
　　▼ 🗀 Yard—Landscaping 2004
▼ 🗀 Special Occasions
　▼ 🗀 2003
　　▼ 🗀 Crystal Ball
　▼ 🗀 2004
　　▼ 🗀 Crave Party
　　▼ 🗀 New Years
　▼ 🗀 2005
　　▼ 🗀 Rob's 40th Birthday
▼ 🗀 Vacations
　▼ 🗀 2003
　　▼ 🗀 Disneyland—July
　　▼ 🗀 Maui—October
　▼ 🗀 2004
　　▼ 🗀 Oahu with Tammy—November
　▼ 🗀 2005
　　▼ 🗀 Kauai with Rob—November
　　▼ 🗀 New York with Rob—May
　　▼ 🗀 Palm Springs with Rob—December
　　▼ 🗀 Phoenix with Rob—March
　　▼ 🗀 San Diego with Rob—April
　　▼ 🗀 Victoria, B.C. with Rob—June

◆ Holidays: By making my Christmas folder part of the Holidays folder, I now have a place to store photos from other holidays. For example, in the future I might want to add a subfile for Easter or Thanksgiving and further subfiles within each of those based on the year. I would model that file structure on the one I used for my Christmas folder.

◆ Professional Work Photos: I didn't change the structure here; rather, I just renamed the folder to be more specific.

◆ Projects: Using a broader name than House Projects will enable me to add subfiles for non-house-related projects to this folder in the future. Further, I divided this Projects folder into Inside and Outside folders, since I always have so many projects going on around my home. I created a subfile for each individual project, and labeled it with the date of the project.

◆ Special Occasions: The Special Occasions folder replaced my previous Events folder. Further, I chose to divide these occasions by year and, within each year, to create a subfile labeled with the name of the event as well as the month it took place.

◆ Vacations: I structured the Vacations folder similar to how I structured the Special Occasions folder, by creating folders by year and then subfiles for each location I vacationed, the person I went with, and the month I went. I retained the original folder name of Vacations because I felt that it was still appropriate.

Naming Conventions

The next two examples will show different naming conventions that can be used when organizing digital photos into folders. Using my Christmas 2004 folder as an example, you can see that I've named each photo starting with the words "Christmas 2004," the same as the folder name. I've then used the "—" to separate those words from the rest of the name. In a few cases, I also included how old my nieces were at the time the photos were taken, so that I won't have to figure this out in the future.

___ Christmas 2004—Anna & Maggie.jpg
___ Christmas 2004—Anna 3.5 years.jpg
___ Christmas 2004—Anna Ice Skating 2.jpg
___ Christmas 2004—Anna Ice Skating.jpg
___ Christmas 2004—Anna in Boots 3.5 years.jpg
___ Christmas 2004—Anna, Sally, Maggie Ice Skating.jpg
___ Christmas 2004—Bailey Under Tree, Eyes Open.jpg
___ Christmas 2004—Bailey Unter Tree, Eyes Closed.jpg
___ Christmas 2004—Dad, Ceil, Maggie, Anna.jpg
___ Christmas 2004—Laura & Dad.jpg
___ Christmas 2004—Laura, Maggie, Anna.jpg
___ Christmas 2004—Laura, Sarah, Ceil.jpg
___ Christmas 2004—Maggie & Anna.jpg
___ Christmas 2004—Maggie 6.5 years.jpg
___ Christmas 2004—Maggie Ice Skating.jpg
___ Christmas 2004—Nik, Bailey, Dad, Fred.jpg
___ Christmas 2004—Nik, Ceil, Fred.jpg
___ Christmas 2004—Sarah & Fred.jpg
___ Christmas 2004—Scott, Sally, Maggie, Anna 2.jpg
___ Christmas 2004—Scott, Sally, Maggie, Anna.jpg

The second example of photo-naming conventions uses my Mozart folder. Instead of starting each photo's name with the year, I decided to start with Mozart's name, then the date, and finally the activity.

___ Mozart—2001 August—Under Sun Umbrella.jpg
___ Mozart—2003 December—Christmas with Laura.jpg
___ Mozart—2003 November—with Laura at Rosie's.jpg
___ Mozart—2004 November—with Kittens.jpg
___ Mozart—2005 January—Snow 1.jpg
___ Mozart—2005 January—Snow 2.jpg
___ Mozart—2005 January—Snow 3.jpg

Storing Photos on CDs and DVDs

Transferring and storing photos on CDs or DVDs is an excellent way to preserve your memories. Be sure to make two copies, one that you can put away for safekeeping and another that can be used as a working copy, if necessary.

Be very careful when labeling or handling your CDs or DVDs. You don't want to touch the surface or bend them, nor do you want to expose them to extreme heat, humidity, or light—all of which can destroy their content. And you shouldn't store them horizontally if you're planning to store them for a long period of time (i.e., years).

Be sure to label all of your discs, but be careful: one of the worst things you can do to a disc is to write on it with a sharp point. Instead, use a non-solvent-based felt-tip permanent marker. You don't want to scratch the label side of the disc either.

If you plan to store photos on CDs or DVDs for a long period of time, consider the fact that this storage medium may not be around in the future. Just 10 years ago, 5.25-inch floppy disks were widely used to store data, and today you'd be hard pressed to find a computer that can even read them.

You may also want to consider that CDs and DVDs have a "life expectancy." The higher their quality, the longer they'll last. For archival purposes, it's recommended that you use discs with a gold metal reflective layer. This is because gold is one of the most reflective elements on earth. Delkin Devices sells archival gold CDs and markers for CDs and DVDs.

Photo Organizing Software

If the task still seems overwhelming, you may want to find a software package that will help you organize your photos. Some resources include the following:

ACDSee: www.acdsystem.com (Windows and Macintosh)

Adobe Photoshop Album: www.adobe.com (Windows)

CompuPic: www.photodex.com (Windows)

IMatch: www.photools.com (Windows)

iPhoto: www.apple.com (Macintosh)

Picasa: www.picasa.com (Windows)

Web-based Digital Photo Albums

If you don't want to spend the time to print your digital photos and make your own photo album or scrapbook, let PhotoWorks do it for you. Visit www.photoworks.com.

NON-PHOTO MEMORABILIA

Non-photo memorabilia comes in all shapes and sizes. It's not possible to store keepsakes such as trophies, a child's special outfit, or an art project in a photo album or scrapbook, so more creative solutions are necessary.

Everyone has various keepsakes that have special meaning to them. But if most of your keepsakes are packed away in boxes that you never open, chances are that you're not enjoying or honoring those special items—as I realized when my grandpa died (see chapter 4).

Which keepsakes provide you with memories that you always want to cherish? These are the items you should take the time to organize.

Tips for Storing Non-Photo Memorabilia

1. **Use a shadow box to capture a special moment in time.** For example, to commemorate the birth of a child, you could include such items as a birth announcement, a hospital wristband, a hospital hat, a special outfit, and a special gift the baby received.

2. **Take a photo.** If your child has created lots of art projects of the three-dimensional variety, take a photo and store that instead. It will take up a lot less room, and the memory will still be there. If you can't let go of everything in that way, hold on to a few special pieces that you may even pass back to your child when he or she is grown up.

3. **Display it.** I once had a client who had a very special set of china given to her by her grandma. She had stored it for many years in a sideboard in her living room. Her house was very small, and she was desperate for any space she could find to store things. The china was taking up a lot of space, yet it was never used, but she simply couldn't part with it. Our solution? We boxed up all of the china in special china crates, except for a cup and saucer and a plate. These three items were placed on a shelf in her living room, where she could now see and honor the china each day.

4. Frame it. Keeping a lot of your children's clothes? Rather than packing them all away in a box, you could take a piece of material from each, and mat and frame them instead. That way you could enjoy them every day.

5. Hang it. Do your children have lots of ribbons they've won through different athletic events or academic achievements? Attach the ribbons to a nice piece of fabric, such as velour, with a safety pin.

6. Store it. If you're holding on to your children's possessions to pass along to them when they're adults, designate a box for each child's items and add to it as necessary. This eliminates the need to sort through it again later.

I sit here today and write the final chapter of this book on what would have been my mom's 67th birthday. I think the book is a fitting tribute to her and those nine words she used to say: "You can't take it with you when you go." Since my mom's death more than 20 years ago, one thing I've learned is that "It's not about the stuff."

The memories I treasure come mostly from the photos I cherish rather than from the memorabilia I kept. Today, I do my best every day to bring into my life only things that serve a purpose and have meaning for me. When I shop, I shop with a purpose. Everything I bring into my home is given a specific place there; if I don't know where that place will be, I don't make the purchase. It's hard to resist the urge to buy things I like, but I know that if they don't have a place in my home, they'll end up becoming clutter.

As you use the 10-step process to organize your home and life, here's some important advice to keep in mind:

◆ Sorting, as painful as it may be, is a critical step in organizing any area of your home. You simply can't create an organized space or system without knowing what you need to organize.

◆ Purging gives you the space for future treasures you'll accumulate. If something no longer has value to you, or you don't use or honor it, let it go.

◆ Many times the reason we hold on to something is that there's a memory attached to it. But if the memory is packed away in a box so that you never see it, what is it truly worth to you? If it truly has meaning to you, find a way to display it so that you can honor it each day.

◆ Maintenance is and will be an ongoing project. After you finish organizing a room in your home or your entire house, maintenance is the step that keeps your home organized.

+ There's no right or wrong way to be organized. Being organized is about creating a space where you can find everything you need, when you need it. There are many different levels of being organized, and you need to determine the one that best suits your lifestyle.

+ Living an organized lifestyle is a choice you make.

If you want to eliminate chaos and lead a more peaceful and organized life, following the 10-step process I've created will help you get there. I wish you the greatest success in all of your organizing projects!

SHOPPING RESOURCES

ORGANIZING PRODUCTS FOR THE HOME

Here's how to contact the stores we used for the projects in this book. To see if there's a location in your area, visit the store's Web site.

Cushy Cupboards
www.cushycupboards.com

Empire Shelving
206-353-1254
www.empireshelving.com

Ikea
800-434-IKEA
www.ikea.com

Lillian Vernon
800-901-9291
www.lillianvernon.com

Onrax
866-637-8828
www.onrax.com
Holds up to 500 pounds per 4'×8' unit.

Organize-Everything
800-600-9817
www.organize-everything.com

Pull-Outs Plus
800-746-5455
www.pull-outsplus.com

ORGANIZING PRODUCTS FOR PHOTOS AND MEMORABILIA

Archival Methods
www.archivalmethods.com
Photo boxes, slide storage, binders, albums, enclosures, envelopes, portfolios, CD and DVD storage, and more

Craft Storage
www.craftstorage.com
Scrapbook storage, photo index cards, photo totes, negative storage, acid-free file folders

Creative Memories
www.creativememories.com
Scrapbook albums and accessories

Delkin
www.delkin.com
Archival gold CDs and markers for CDs and DVDs

Exposures
www.exposuresonline.com
Photo boxes, photo albums, scrapbooks, magazine files, art files

Gaylord
www.gaylordmart.com
Acid and lignin-free photo, CD, and negative storage, map and rolled drawing storage, archival glue, pens

Get Smart Products
www.getsmartproducts.com
Portfolio cases and books, scrapbook supplies, photo albums, photo boxes, slide storage, APS photo storage and cases, CD storage

Metal Edge
www.metaledgeinc.com
Archival CD storage, photo and negative storage, marking pens and pencils, portfolios

Photoworks
www.photoworks.com
Online photo albums and scrapbooks

Your Family Legacy
www.webyfl.com
Archival boxes and storage, scrapbook supplies, acid-free pens, pH testing pens

OTHER RESOURCES

Renee Bassetti
www.reneebassetti.com
206-467-6549
Renee Bassetti, fine shirt maker and clothier, custom-designed the shirt Laura wears in the photo on the cover.

Audrey Beaulac Style
www.audreybeaulacstyle.com
206-351-7847
Image consultant who worked with me for the cover of this book and helped me clear out my closet.

CheckFree
www.checkfree.com
CheckFree is a bill-paying service you can subscribe to for a small fee, thus eliminating all of the paper bills you receive.

Culinary Parts
www.culinaryparts.com
866-PART-HELP
Culinary Parts can help you find a part for that broken appliance in your kitchen.

Eliminate Chaos
www.eliminatechaos.com
425-670-2551
Our Web site offers many resources, including Organizing and Customizing with Microsoft Outlook, *which can help you organize your e-mail for maximum productivity.*

Freecycle
www.freecycle.org
Freecycle is an online service that allows you to post things you want to give away, and get responses from people who want them. It's active in more than 2,000 communities across the country.

Jennifer Humes
www.clutterqueen.com
214-906-9648
Laundry Lessons—A DVD on how to organize your laundry room.

FINDING A PROFESSIONAL ORGANIZER

I f you would like to enlist the help of an expert, here are several groups that can help you locate a professional organizer or organizing consultant in your area. Organizers work in all areas of the home as well as with businesses.

National Association of Professional Organizers (NAPO)

www.napo.net

Founded in 1985, NAPO is the authority on organizing, with more than 3,700 members throughout the United States, Canada, and other countries around the world. The NAPO Web site features a free, automated referral system that enables you to find an expert in your geographic area who specializes in the type of organizing you need.

National Study Group on Chronic Disorganization (NSGCD)

www.nsgcd.org

NSGCD provides education on chronic disorganization and referrals to experts who specialize in helping chronically disorganized clients and those with additional needs due to physical and mental disabilities.

Professional Organizers in Canada (POC)

www.organizersincanada.com

Founded in 2001, POC has more than 300 members working throughout the Canadian provinces. The POC Web site features a free, automated referral system that enables you to find an expert in your geographic area.

ABOUT THE AUTHOR

Laura Leist is an organizing consultant and owner of a Northwest-based company, Eliminate Chaos, which provides organizing services to individuals in their homes, small businesses, and corporations. Laura has a BS in management information systems and a certificate in software product management. She was recognized as one of Washington State's "40 Under 40 Entrepreneurs" in 2001. Her Extreme Makeovers have been featured on the television programs *Northwest Afternoon, Evening Magazine,* and *Seattle Live,* as well as radio programs. Laura has also been featured in print in *Northwest Home and Garden, Remodel Seattle, King County Journal,* and the *Puget Sound Business Journal.*

Prior to forming Eliminate Chaos, Laura was director of product management for several companies, as well as a business-process consultant. She also taught technology courses worldwide. Laura's award-winning organization, process design, and re-engineering work have been recognized at the corporate level, and she was also named a Safeco Surety Employee of the Year.

Laura is a regular presenter of organizing seminars at Ikea and also speaks to a variety of groups nationally. She has established a name for herself in the organizing industry, receiving various commendations from her peers at the National Association of Professional Organizers (NAPO), where she serves on the board of directors. She also serves on the board of the NW Next Leaders Council and is a member of the National Speaker's Association (NSA) as well as the Master Builders Association.

Laura is the author of two self-published tip books: *Organizing and Customizing with Microsoft Outlook* and *Eliminate Chaos . . . In Your Home* (available at her Web site: EliminateChaos.com). Friends and family used to tease Laura every year at her annual BBQ about "labeling" all of the drinks—now they freely admit that she managed to turn labeling into a profitable organizing business!